BRIEF THERAPY
FOR ADOLESCENT
DEPRESSION

Scott Temple, PhD

Clinical Assistant Professor
Division of Child and Adolescent Psychiatry
Department of Psychiatry
Kansas University Medical Center

Professional Resource Press
Sarasota, Florida

Published by
Professional Resource Press
(An imprint of Professional Resource Exchange, Inc.)
Post Office Box 15560
Sarasota, FL 34277-1560

Printed in the United States of America

Copyright © 1997 by Professional Resource Exchange, Inc.

All rights reserved

The copy editor was Brian Fogarty, the managing editor was Debra Fink, and the production coordinator was Laurie Girsch.

Library of Congress Cataloging-in-Publication Data

Temple, Scott, date.
    Brief therapy for adolescent depression / Scott Temple.
        p.   cm. -- (Practitioner's resource series)
    Includes bibliographical references.
    ISBN 1-56887-028-0 (alk. paper)
    1. Depression in adolescence--Treatment. 2. Cognitive therapy for teenagers. 3. Brief psychotherapy for teenagers. I. Title.
II. Series.
RJ506.D4T45   1997
616.85'270651'0835--dc21   97-20410
                                                 CIP

DEDICATION

For Rachel
My wife, best friend, and teacher for 25 years;
And for our sons,
David and Jesse.

ACKNOWLEDGMENTS

I would like to thank Wayne Bowers, PhD, of the Department of Psychiatry at the University of Iowa. Much of what I know about cognitive therapy I learned from Wayne, and I also benefited from his review of an earlier draft of this manuscript. This is a better work thanks to Wayne's many helpful comments and suggestions. I am also grateful for the chance I have had to study intensively with Ivan Boszormenyi-Nagy, MD. Dr. Nagy has been instrumental in the development of my own thinking about families, about psychotherapy, and about the proper motivations for working with people.

I owe a particular debt of gratitude to the many depressed and unhappy young people with whom I have worked over the years. I would like to think that this brief guide is part of a larger effort that will eventually lead to more effective treatments for depression in young people than we have today.

Finally, I would like to thank my students in the Psychiatry Department at Kansas University Medical Center. All helped shape my thinking at our weekly adolescent therapy conference; but, I would like to especially thank Drs. Diane Buckingham, David Ermer, Mark Kerekes, and Larry McDonald.

PREFACE TO THE SERIES

As a publisher of books, cassettes, and continuing education programs, the Professional Resource Press and Professional Resource Exchange, Inc. strive to provide mental health professionals with highly applied resources that can be used to enhance clinical skills and expand practical knowledge.

All titles in the *Practitioner's Resource Series* are designed to provide important new information on topics of vital concern to psychologists, clinical social workers, marriage and family therapists, psychiatrists, and other mental health professionals.

Although the focus and content of each book in this series will be quite different, there will be notable similarities:

1. Each title in the series will address a timely topic of critical clinical importance.

2. The target audience for each title will be practicing mental health professionals. Our authors were chosen for their ability to provide concrete, "how-to-do-it" guidance to colleagues who are trying to increase their competence in dealing with complex clinical problems.

3. The information provided in these books will represent "state-of-the-art" information and techniques derived from both clinical experience and empirical research. Each of these guide books will include references and resources for

those who wish to pursue more advanced study of the discussed topic.

4. The authors will provide numerous case studies, specific recommendations for practice, and the types of "nitty-gritty" details that clinicians need before they can incorporate new concepts and procedures into their practices.

We feel that one of the unique assets of the Professional Resource Press is that all of its editorial decisions are made by mental health professionals. The publisher, all editorial consultants, and all reviewers are practicing psychologists, marriage and family therapists, clinical social workers, and psychiatrists.

If there are other topics you would like to see addressed in this series, please let me know.

Lawrence G. Ritt, Publisher

ABSTRACT

This work adapts cognitive therapy for use in treating de-pressed adolescents. It is intended for use with young people, roughly between 13 and 18, who meet diagnostic criteria for major depression, but whose features and comorbid conditions do not suggest a need for hospitalization.

Adaptations of cognitive therapy for use with young people are necessary for two reasons. First, there are cognitive differences between adults and adolescents that may influence the young person's ability to distance from his or her own thinking, so as to view thoughts in relative, rather than absolute, terms. Second, young people are developmentally embedded in the family of origin, and therefore family members are often highly implicated in the maintenance, if not origins, of major depressive episodes. Effective treatment rarely can be conducted without intervening with the family.

The author originally developed this manual as a training vehicle for graduate students in psychology, nursing, and social work, as well as psychiatry residents. It is hoped that experienced clinicians wishing to learn a new modality for treating depressed young people will also find this guide useful.

TABLE OF CONTENTS

STRUCTURE OF PSYCHOTHERAPY SESSIONS ON A SESSION-BY-SESSION BASIS *(Continued)*

BRIEF THERAPY
FOR ADOLESCENT
DEPRESSION

INTRODUCTION

Despite an increasing recognition of the severity and consequences of adolescent depression, there remains little in the way
of scientifically validated psychotherapy or pharmacotherapy in the
treatment of depressed young people. Current treatments typically
involve the development of downward extensions of adult treatment for depression (Mufson et al., 1993; Wilkes et al., 1994).
More specifically, cognitive therapy and interpersonal therapy for
adolescent depression appear promising, especially in light of their
demonstration of at least some efficacy in treating adult depression
(Elkin, 1994). Such factors as differing cognitive capacities, as
well as the different role of the family for young people, must be
addressed in attempting to adapt an adult psychotherapy model for
work with depressed young people. The difficulties in making
this shift from adult psychotherapy models to ones appropriate for
young people are perhaps partially responsible for the relative
paucity of specific treatments for adolescent depression. Earlier
controversies as to the existence and nature of youth depression
have also contributed to the lagging development of effective
treatments.

While results of epidemiological studies are ambiguous, con-
servative prevalence estimates suggest that 2% to 4% of young
people may suffer from a severe depression at any given time
(Kashani et al., 1987; Stark, 1990). Depressed young people may

1

be at greater risk of an eventual diagnosis of bipolar disorder (Ryan, 1992); and their episodes are likely to be prolonged, wreaking havoc on their life adjustment, including putting them at greater risk for suicide (King & Noshpitz, 1991).

Nonetheless, treatment efforts for depression in young persons lag considerably behind those for adult depression. With regard to adolescents, Moreau et al. (1991) noted that "Despite the widespread clinical use of various treatment modalities, there is not one published controlled clinical trial of the efficacy of any psychotherapy in the treatment of adolescents diagnosed as depressed, according to *DSM-III-R* criteria" (p. 642). Ryan (1992), in a review of drug therapy for child and adolescent depression, observed that "In adolescents there are not yet any controlled studies of either pharmacological or psychological treatments of major depressive disorder that demonstrate the superiority of active treatment over placebo" (p. 230).

PHARMACOTHERAPIES

Pharmacotherapies for youth depression have continued to provide disappointing results in controlled studies (Rosenberg, Holttum, & Gershon, 1994). This includes a failure "to demonstrate that TCA's (tricyclic antidepressants) are superior to placebos in the treatment of childhood and adolescent depression" (p. 60). Despite this reported lack of scientific evidence to support tricyclic use, "clinicians continue to prescribe these agents in the belief that future studies will show that higher plasma levels or correctly adjusted doses of antidepressants will be effective" (p. 61).

Geller (1991) sounded a cautionary note regarding the use of tricyclic antidepressants with young persons, due to the lack of demonstrated treatment efficacy in controlled outcome trials and to cardiotoxic effects. Geller urges the development of psychosocial approaches in treating depression in young persons. Further evidence of the need for nonmedication alternatives to treatment is provided by Puig-Antich et al. (1985b) in a generally favorable study of tricyclic antidepressants. They observed that although cognitive symptoms of depression in children returned to baseline following a trial of TCA's, ongoing relationship problems with family and friends remained.

Newer antidepressant drugs, including the specific seratonin reuptake inhibitors (SSRIs), show promise of being of help in treating youth depression. Nonetheless, a recent text on pharmacotherapy in children and adolescents concludes with regard to the widely used drug Prozac that "Efficacy and safety have not yet been established for children and adolescents, but its clinical use in this population has been increasing" (Rosenberg et al.,1994, p. 105). With regard to the still newer drugs Zoloft and Paxil, they conclude that "Because of the recent introduction of sertraline and paroxetine into the U.S. market, there are no available data for children and adolescents" (p. 105). In a more recent review, Birmaher et al. (1996) state that while cognitive-behavior therapy is a useful initial treatment for youth depression, "SSRIs may also be a good alternative initial treatment for depressed children and adolescents" (p. 1580).

Relatively few controlled outcome studies of psychosocial interventions are found in the literature. Kutcher and Marton (1989) stated that because the understanding that adolescent depression is relatively isomorphic to adult depression, treatment efforts with adolescents have involved downward extensions of adult models. As such, behavioral and cognitive behavioral treatments generally have led the way in terms of outcome studies. These have principally involved group-administered treatments for adolescents (Lewinsohn & Clarke, 1990; Reynolds & Coats, 1986) and children (Stark, 1990; Stark, Raffaelle, & Reysa, 1994; Stark, Reynolds, & Kaslow, 1987).

Individually oriented treatment models are just beginning to be explored in terms of potential for eventual outcome studies using manualized treatments. As reported previously, no controlled outcome studies using individually administered treatments have thus far been done. Again, these models are based on existing treatments that have demonstrated efficacy with adult unipolar, nonpsychotic depression. In particular, cognitive therapy (Reinecke, 1992; Schrodt, 1992; Wilkes et al., 1994; Wilkes & Rush, 1988) and interpersonal therapy (Moreau et al., 1991; Mufson et

3

al., 1993) have generated interest as downward extensions of their adult counterparts.

COGNITIVE THERAPY

The basics of cognitive therapy are well known and are available in many books, chapters, and articles (Beck, 1976; Beck et al., 1979; Beck & Young, 1985). The hallmark of this theory is the assumption that experience is mediated by thought. As such, one's behavioral and affective responses to life situations become intelligible when one's relatively automatized, stereotypic cognitions are verbalized. Beck found characteristic patterns of distortions in the thought processes of patients suffering major depression. In particular, he noted the emergence of the cognitive triad, involving generally negative appraisals of oneself, one's interpersonal world, and one's future.

Therapeutic work initially focuses on helping patients monitor for the presence of automatic thoughts, defined as quick, fleeting thoughts that pop into the edges of awareness. These thoughts are generally quite believable to the depressed person and go unchallenged. They exert predictably depressive effects on the mood and behavior of depressed persons. Negative automatic thoughts tend to recede with successful treatment in adults, whether through psychotherapy or medication.

After the patient's automatic thoughts are identified, through self-monitoring homework and work in therapy sessions, the patient is taught to distance himself or herself from these thoughts, and to test them empirically for their relative accuracy or distortion. The therapist maintains a socratic, guided-discovery posture, in which patients are enlisted as collaborators in studying their own thoughts, moods, and behaviors, and in generating more adaptive cognitions. Behavioral techniques such as activity scheduling are intended to alter the patient's appraisals, not just his or her behavior.

Once symptom relief is achieved, cognitive therapy attempts to achieve a prophylactic effect (Hollon, 1990) in modifying underlying schemas (Young, 1994). Schemas are regarded as patterns of automatic thoughts that form core beliefs, generally related to earlier developmental eras of the patient's life (Guidano, 1987; Guidano & Liotti, 1983; Liotti, 1987). These may take the form of "if-then" propositions, or, on a deeper level, may globally invalidate the worth and lovability of the patient, regardless of his or her accomplishments in life.

Cognitive therapy uses a manualized format in which a specific agenda is followed on a session-by-session basis. Despite this structure, there is still considerable flexibility available to both therapist and patient, regarding which target symptoms and which specific techniques will be the focus of each session. An early emphasis is placed on establishing a viable treatment alliance, in addition to ensuring that mechanisms are in place to frequently elicit patient perceptions of the therapist and therapy. Early in the therapy, the patient is "socialized to the cognitive model" via reading and therapist mini-lectures. Treatment sessions resemble one another in the sense that the general structure of each session is comparable to other sessions (e.g., perceptions of previous sessions are elicited, homework assignments are reviewed, agendas for the current session are established, homework assignments for the next session are developed, and reviews of the current session are conducted).

Although cognitive therapy is a reasonably well validated treatment method for adult unipolar depression, there is no research support for the use of cognitive therapy with depressed adolescents. However, there are suggestions that modifications in the standard techniques may allow the model to be effectively used with adolescents. Specific modifications have been proposed in two areas: tailoring techniques to the developmental level of young persons, and including the family in treatment (Wilkes et al., 1994).

Several reports address the application of the cognitive model to young people (Reinecke, 1992; Schrodt, 1992; Wilkes et al., 1994; Wilkes & Rush, 1988). Wilkes and Rush presented four cases in which cognitive therapy was modified in two key areas for use with adolescent depression. First, the authors argue against using cognitive techniques that encourage identifying and disputing cognitive distortions. They suggest a focus on building alternative thinking, such as "What's another way of looking at this?" Second, these authors suggest the use of structural family therapy (Minuchin, 1974; Minuchin & Fishman, 1981) with this population.

Reinecke (1992), in a paper dealing with applications of cognitive therapy with preadolescents, advocated blending analytically derived techniques into cognitive therapy. For example, he cited the use of Donald Winnicott's "squiggly test" as a means of engaging children in drawings, while simultaneously exploring their thought processes (Winnicott, 1958). Reinecke also noted that he uses these techniques within a cognitive framework, rather than within psychoanalytic or interpretive frameworks.

Schrodt (1992) also addressed the issue of modifications in the cognitive model to meet the developmental needs of the younger patient. He noted that egocentricity and lack of the capacity to "think about thinking" conspire against successfully implementing the adult model with younger patients. These observations dovetail with Wilkes and Rush (1988) in their recognition of the need to focus on alternative ways of construing a situation, rather than on a higher-order set of cognitive processes.

A body of literature exists that may provide relatively simple, reasonably well researched techniques that can supplement cognitive therapy with adolescents. Problem-solving approaches to adjustment and therapy have been derived from a developmental perspective in which components of adequate social problem-solving are noted at each developmental era. Appropriate interventions based on the developmental issues of each era have been empirically identified and implemented.

PROBLEM-SOLVING APPROACHES

Problem-solving approaches include developmental and treatment research (D'Zurilla, 1988; A. M. Nezu, C. M. Nezu, & Perri, 1989; Spivack, Platt, & Shure, 1976; Spivack & Shure, 1974). To date, no comparable literature has been developed for internalizing disorders, particularly adolescent depression. Nonetheless, components of a problem-solving approach are part of both the cognitive model and the cognitive-behavioral models (Lewinsohn & Clarke, 1990; Stark, 1990; Stark et al., 1994). Appropriate modifications of cognitive therapy to suit the developmental needs of younger patients may be found in the problem-solving literature.

The capacity to solve interpersonal problems has long been regarded as a hallmark of successful adjustment across the life cycle. Spivack et al. (1976) provide a research-based model of the components of successful interpersonal problem-solving. As it relates to adolescents, their model proposes that the following capacities are most critical for adequate adjustment: means-ends thinking, alternative-solution thinking, and perspective-taking skills.

Spivack et al. define means-ends thinking as "the ability to orient oneself to and conceptualize the step-by-step means of moving toward a goal" (p. 83). This skill requires planning, anticipating obstacles, and time-consciousness. They note that "Adolescents demonstrating a variety of behavioral maladjustments exhibit some deficiencies in means-ends cognition when compared with equivalent groups not demonstrating such aberrance" (pp. 88-89).

Alternative thinking involves the capacity to generate a variety of alternatives to a problem's solution. Spivack and Shure (1974) showed this to be a significant predictor of future adjustment in young children. They also found alternative thinking to be a feature of adolescent adjustment. They noted that "Whether or not a child considers consequences to a given interpersonal act, the key indicator of aberrant behavior is lack of ability to think of different ways to go about solving an interpersonal problem" (Spivack et al., 1976, p. 51). Similar findings were obtained for populations of disturbed adolescents. This function is customarily assessed using a variety of paper-and-pencil or observational measures (D'Zurilla, 1988). A variation on this theme is found in the widely used cognitive technique of asking a young person "What's another way of looking at it?" Wilkes and Rush (1988) wrote that encouragement of alternative ways of looking at problem situations may prove more fruitful than attempting to train adolescents to critically evaluate their thoughts for errors and distortions.

Finally, perspective-taking skills involve training young persons to understand how others may experience a problem situation. Chandler (1973) provided evidence that children with externalizing disorders showed behavioral improvement when systematically trained in perspective-taking skills through role playing. Spivack et al. (1976) found that the presence of perspective-taking skills separated normal adolescents from a patient population.

Another elaboration of the problem-solving approach is provided by A. M. Nezu et al. (1989). Their model involves a five-component process: problem orientation, problem definition and formulation, generation of alternatives, decision making, and solution implementation and verification. "Treatment within this perspective involves both the assessment and amelioration of deficits in any or all of these five problem-solving processes" (A. M. Nezu et al., 1989, p. 248). Their work involved outcome studies with major unipolar depression in adults, and lends itself to structured, time-limited group formats or individual, open-ended treatments. Its applications with adolescents are speculative.

Although the approach defined by A. M. Nezu et al. (1989), as well as D'Zurilla (1988) dovetails with key features of cognitive therapy, both urge therapists to make their approach primary in any effort to blend it with other methods.

For example, in reviewing their problem orientation component, similarities to cognitive therapy become clear. Both systems recognize that failed problem solving can result from either deficits or distortions in thinking. In particular, a young person could have adequate social problem-solving skills at baseline, but not during a depressive episode. The depressive thinking found in the cognitive triad could lead to negative outcomes in interpersonal encounters. At the same time, longstanding deficits in social problem-solving skills may predate the onset of a current depression. In the latter case, treatment may involve training new cognitive and behavioral skills, rather than clearing away the depressive barriers and invoking old skills. This approach involves two things at this stage: dampening the intense affects that impede problem identification, and mobilizing the patient's hope for their ability to address important life issues.

The proposed means of generating alternative solutions to problems is highly structured, and is of considerable interest in working with adolescents. A. M. Nezu et al. advocate encouraging a joint nonevaluative effort to generate all options that occur to either the patient or the therapist. At this stage, patients are encouraged to suspend judgment regarding the various alternatives and combine them into new alternatives.

Once a list of alternatives has been generated, the patient is taken through a detailed process of evaluating each one separately. Then the decision can be made to identify the one most likely to solve the problem. The remaining work involves implementation and evaluation of the strategies employed.

While the preceding problem-solving therapist (PST) authors (D'Zurilla, 1988; A. M. Nezu et al., 1989) argue for making other treatment methods subordinate to their own, the overall framework of cognitive therapy can be maintained while using parts of the problem-solving approaches described earlier. In particular, due to the difficulty many adolescents may have in distancing themselves from their own thought processes and scrutinizing their automatic thoughts for the presence of distortions and errors, generating alternatives may well be a better way of reaching these young people. Similarly, because family disturbances are common among depressed youth, perspective-taking skills may be effectively combined in working with these young people and their families.

Of added interest for work with depressed youth is the concern of the PST theorists with factors that impede adequate problem-solving development. They recognize that cognitive deficits lead to a restricted, stereotyped interpersonal problem-solving repertoire. They also recognize that affective states can hinder young people in utilizing a more functional range of problem-solving skills. More germane for depression is the finding of Spivack et al. (1976) that although both impulsive and inhibited young people demonstrate fewer problem-solving skills than normal youths, the inhibited youths demonstrate the poorest capacity for alternative thinking and means-ends thinking skills. To the degree that clinically depressed young persons mirror the inhibited children in the Spivack et al. studies, they may also be deficient in problem-solving abilities. It remains to be studied whether major depression, alone or in concert with other comorbid conditions, is characterized by cognitive deficits or by depressive inhibition of more adequate baseline skills.

FAMILY THERAPY

The consensus among both cognitive and cognitive-behavioral investigators is that family involvement of some kind is necessary for successful treatment of depressed adolescents. However, the attention to detail in the treatment of the individual adolescent has not translated into a comparably detailed focus on family interventions. Perhaps because of paradigmatic dissimilarities, family and cognitive-behavioral models have been poorly integrated (Leslie, 1988).

Family therapy models are abundant and quite diverse from one another (Gurman & Kniskern, 1991; Nichols, 1984; Nichols & Schwartz, 1995). As noted earlier, only one paper specifically identifies a current family therapy model for integration with cognitive therapy (Wilkes & Rush, 1988). Most of the remaining authors who include families, do so solely for the purpose of educating families about depression, for eliciting the family members' perceptions of the depressed young person, and to enlist the family as auxiliary therapists in implementing the individual treatment plan in the home.

Lewinsohn and Clarke (1990) compared a group treatment condition for adolescents without parental inclusion with one in which parental inclusion in a parents' group was added. Partly because of difficulties enlisting parents in the treatment, the effects were not significantly different for the two treatment conditions. However, the trends were toward a greater therapeutic impact using the combined approach. It is important to add that although parents were involved in this study, they were not directly included in meetings with the depressed adolescent.

Braswell (1991) has spoken to the need to integrate families into a cognitive-behavioral treatment. She noted that "The dearth of cognitive-behavioral outcome studies addressing childhood depression is particularly difficult to understand, given the well-documented efficacy of this approach with adults" (p. 332). She then noted that "The available interventions for childhood depression, cognitive-behavioral or otherwise, have tended to exclude parents from active participation in treatment" (p. 332). She then advocates inclusion of parents in the assessment, such as eliciting perceptions of their child and assessing marital and family discord. Braswell acknowledges the benefit in educating parents in relatively less impaired families about child and adolescent disorders such as depression. With respect to treatment issues, Braswell states that "At a minimum, parents should be taught to prompt and reinforce the child's use of newly trained skills" (p. 340). She briefly describes essentially cognitive interventions for modifying parental cognitive distortions and misperceptions regarding their child.

Kendall and Morris (1991) go beyond Braswell by noting "The potential utility of a diagnostic category that identifies the family (not the child) as maladjusted or disordered" (p. 778). They further raise the compelling question of whether children with or without disturbed parents and impaired families would respond differentially to psychotherapeutic interventions.

Addressing the issue of the superiority of family versus individual treatment approaches, Fauber and Long (1991) wrote that "Although family-oriented approaches to child treatment appear to have gained popularity, this movement has flourished largely in the absence of any conclusive evidence that family-based approaches are superior to individual therapy in the treatment of children's psychological problems" (p. 813). They make the point that although both individual and family approaches can claim to be somewhat effective, neither can claim greater efficacy than the other. Fauber and Long provide tentative clinical guidelines for decision making about family involvement in child therapy. Their recommendations include:

1. Determination of the degree to which the family has a direct role in the etiology and maintenance of the problem. They noted that this is poorly established with regard to internalizing disorders such as depression.
2. Since research presently offers no guidelines regarding the specific form of family involvement warranted in a given situation, family involvement should be limited to altering specific interactions that produce or maintain the child's dysfunction.
3. Family members should be enlisted as allies or confederates in the treatment process. This may take the form of

extending "the work of therapy into the home environment by providing additional support and reinforcement for alternative behaviors, increased understanding of the problems, or consistent modeling of more adaptive behaviors, thought patterns, and so forth" (Fauber & Long, 1991, p. 818).

4. Establishing when family inclusion may be contraindicated, such as intractable family conflict, abuse, or other situations where the child may require the shelter and safety of an exclusive relationship with the therapist.

5. Resisting either/or thinking, and flexibly incorporating both individual and family therapy modalities as indicated.

Although Kendall and Morris (1991) advocate eventual comparisons of the two models in treatment outcome studies, it is part of the present effort to include the family in the treatment of the depressed adolescent in a manner that allows for combined individual and family intervention foci.

One particularly acute difficulty, as reflected in the cognitive and cognitive-behavioral literature, is shifting between two essentially different paradigms for conceptualizing disorders and for intervening. Leslie (1988) writes that systems and cognitive-behavioral paradigms are only partially compatible. Other difficulties are practical as much as theoretical. It is difficult enough to intervene effectively using a cognitive-behavioral model with individual adolescents. Is it asking too much of a therapist to develop comparable effectiveness in two different modalities, each incorporated into the same treatment? Difficulties with therapist drift from manualized treatments, as well as site differences of treatment effect, were noted in the multicenter National Institute of Mental Health (NIMH) depression study of the 1980s (Elkin, 1994). How much would these thorny difficulties be compounded by the use of two modalities in one treatment effort?

Given the dearth of empirically established guidelines and the heat of the debate in the theoretical literature, what kind of family involvement can be designed to fit into a manualized treatment format?

In this author's opinion, the principles of cognitive and problem-solving therapy are adaptable for work with families. However, modifications in technique, scope, and focus are required for the adaptations to be successful. A blend of these approaches with Minuchin's structural family therapy (Minuchin, 1974) is detailed by Robin and Foster (1989). Their intervention program is for generic parent-adolescent conflict, rather than targeting a specific diagnostic category. Minuchin's approach to family therapy is also incorporated into the work of Wilkes and Rush (1988) and Wilkes et al. (1994), who make an effort to employ structural family therapy specifically for treating adolescent depression.

The Behavioral Family Therapy (BFT) of Mueser and Glynn (1995) shares the most features with the present effort, and appears to be the most adaptable of the existing treatment models for work with depressed adolescents. Chief characteristics of this model include:

1. A psychoeducational focus, oriented toward helping family members develop a nonblaming attitude toward major depression in young people.
2. An emphasis on communication training to decrease negative interchanges between family members.
3. The use of problem-solving strategies to empower families in addressing issues of daily conflict as they arise around the issue of adolescent depression.
4. A prophylactic emphasis, as youth and family members are trained to identify recurrences of major depression early enough to intervene prior to severe impairments in adaptive functioning.

In addition to technical compatibility, the philosophical perspective out of which BFT operates is consistent with the present effort. For example, besides viewing major depression as a nonvolitional entity best constructed as a disorder, BFT adopts a nonblaming stance toward families who may be exacerbating episodes of depression in youth. Mueser and Glynn (1995) cite the literature on expressed emotion in families, and rather convincingly demonstrate that exacerbation *and* relapse rates are impacted by family interaction style. In particular, they describe the impact of families that display critical, hostile, or emotionally overinvolved attitudes toward patients (high expressed emotion). They note that "The predictive utility of expressed emotion appears to be greatest for depression, in which even low levels of criticism are related to an increased likelihood that the patient will relapse" (p. 17). It is speculative at this point whether such increased relapse rates occur with depressed youth, though it would appear to be a logical inference that, if anything, youth may be even more susceptible to the damaging impact of negative interchanges with family members.

While the practitioner using the approach advocated in this guide will be required to weave together individual and family-level interventions, the theoretical and practical similarities of the two levels of intervention should adequately address the issues previously raised. For example, just as cognitive distortions may be targeted for intervention with the individual adolescent, they may also be targeted for family-level interventions. Just as the individual adolescent may focus on problem solving, the same approach may be implemented using the family. Should communication styles or structural issues impede relatively quick individual implementations of problem-solving and cognitive approaches, they may then be targeted for intervention at family level. Family interventions would then be available on an as-needed basis, ranging from relatively less to more intensive. Treatment will confine itself, whenever possible, to the guidelines previously noted (Fauber & Long, 1991). This will involve an individual focus for treatment, with a family involvement in assessment, education, and possibly conjoint problem solving. Communication and structural interventions will therefore be reserved for use on an as-needed basis.

The following notions may serve as guideposts for including families in the treatment of depressed adolescents:

1. The primary focus should remain on the syndrome of major depression, with the individual young person as the index patient.

2. Family members, particularly the parent(s) with whom the young person resides, should be included in the assessment phase.
3. Structured interviews and rating scales should be employed with parents to gauge child and parental psychopathology. Measures of family conflict should be administered to aid in determining the nature and degree of family involvement indicated in the treatment phase.
4. Parents and other relevant family members should be involved in educative interventions. Involvement should provide the family the opportunity to refine their own idiosyncratic interpretations of the index patient's problems. This is conceived as best done through educating the family about the nature of depression in young people, and encouraging matching this information to their own understanding, via a socratic process (Beck et al., 1979).
5. Family involvement in treatment should include a problem-solving focus on specific issues identified by both parents and child, following the strategies suggested in the cognitive and problem-solving literature, as well as the family model detailed in Mueser and Glynn (1995). The therapists' knowledge of systems approaches may come into play in anticipating the interference that triangles, cross-generational coalitions, and detouring may cause (Minuchin, 1974). Communication training will also be used, as needed, when flawed communicative styles impede problem-solving effectiveness within families.
6. Family members should be included in the outcome evaluation of treatment, though Kendall and Morris (1991) have warned that families involved in treatment may provide biased outcome estimates.

MANUALIZED TREATMENT

Finally, a word is in order regarding the use of treatment manuals. The appeal of manualized approaches has grown substantially over the past decade. Treatment manuals are increasingly required for conducting clinical research, and are utilized in

15

the training of both fledgling clinicians and experienced clinicians interested in learning new modalities (Bowers & Temple, 1995). At the same time, the economics of mental health care increasingly has dictated briefer, more focused treatments; the very stuff of manualized treatments. Kendall, MacDonald, and Treadwell (1995) have written that "In the absence of a manualization of the procedures used by these approaches (psychoanalytic) and a lack of research support for their effects, third party and other payers are inclined to steer toward other approaches" (p. 580).

The movement toward manualization, therefore, accomplishes multiple purposes:

1. Relative standardization of treatment conditions for clinical research.
2. Structured vehicles for training clinicians.
3. Vehicles for demonstrating efficacy to third-party payers and consumers.
4. Mechanisms for helping to elevate the standards of care in the field away from treatments that are purely ideologically driven, and toward treatments that have more sound theoretical and technical underpinnings.

There is, however, a seductive appeal to manualized approaches. A treatment manual can create the false illusion that cookbook approaches are contained within the manual's pages, with any and all contingencies neatly outlined for the reader. Even more sobering is the finding of Holloway and Neufeldt (1995) that the quality of the treatment relationship may be impaired when even experienced clinicians attempt to be overly scrupulous in following manualized approaches. The importance of a treatment alliance cannot be overestimated, particularly when working with angry and discouraged young people who are often deeply distrustful of adult helpers. The reader is encouraged to flexibly utilize the approach contained in this volume, always subordinating technique to relationship. In that spirit, this manual hopefully will contribute to improved training of clinicians and improved treatment outcome with adolescent depression.

SUMMARY

Depression is increasingly recognized as a serious problem among young persons. However, few controlled-outcome studies have been conducted on treatments for this population. No studies have ever been reported for individually administered psychotherapies of adolescent depression. While drug studies have been conducted, their results are unimpressive. Treatments that have been proposed for this population have largely been downward extensions of adult-oriented treatments.

Cognitive therapy for adolescents has been advocated as a possibly powerful method for treating depression and for promoting cognitive development in this group. However, it appears unlikely that the cognitive therapy used with adult depressives can be applied to adolescents without modifications. Modifications need to be made based on two factors:

1. The cognitive development of young people.
2. The relative dependency young people maintain with their families.

With regard to adolescent cognitive development, it is posited that the capacity to detach from and observe one's own thinking may be poorly evolved in depressed youth. Although adolescence is an era of explosive growth in cognitive abilities, the ability to "think about thinking," to view one's own perceptions as relative rather than absolute, is likely to be poorly developed. The interpersonal problem-solving literature suggests ways to modify cognitive techniques to increase their effectiveness when working with adolescents. In particular, it is advocated that depressed young people be taught to seek alternative ways of looking at and solving the interpersonal conflicts that are frequently part and parcel of their depression. In other words, the principal locus of disturbance remains in the depressed youth's cognitive appraisal of the situation. Even though objective life circumstances may indeed be very difficult, the cognitive model maintains that it is the young person's stereotypical and rigid thinking, as organized around the cognitive triad, that should be targeted for intervention. In the author's opinion, a concomitant problem-solving focus should also occur. This involves generating alternatives, planning "experiments" to test alternative strategies, and implementing these efforts in vivo, through direct work with the young person and his or her family. While opposite-sex and same-sex friends will not be directly included in therapy, they can be indirectly involved using the traditional cognitive therapy techniques which are detailed in a later section of this guide. Direct and indirect inclusion of significant persons in the young person's life will also allow for the development of more refined and functional perspective-taking skills. Robin and Foster's (1989) program for treating parent-adolescent conflicts dovetails with the components of our individual treatment model, particularly the cognitive and problem-solving interventions. In addition, their inclusion of family communication training and structural interventions adds to the range of interventions available to the therapist. A basic premise of the approach described in this book is that a real world, action-oriented, problem-solving treatment approach will enhance cognitive growth, while simultaneously diminishing a young person's depressive symptoms.

We will now turn our attention to a more detailed exploration of assessment procedures and treatment techniques.

ASSESSMENT OF
ADOLESCENT DEPRESSION

There are disorders of childhood and adolescence that carry the presumption of a biological origin, with contributions from the psychosocial domain. Examples include Attention-Deficit/Hyperactivity Disorder (Barkley, 1990) and Obsessive-Compulsive Disorder (Rapoport, 1989). Depression appears etiologically to be more multifaceted, and has been described as the product of multiple etiological possibilities (Kutcher & Marton, 1989). It is increasingly clear that for at least a subgroup of depressed youth, there is a heightened risk of eventually developing bipolar disorder (Ryan, 1992). Familial factors, presumed to be biological, are also implicated (E. B. Weller & R. Weller, 1984). Additional factors such as early loss, grief, and a host of other psychosocial events are clearly linked to depression and demonstrate that the underpinnings of this disorder are varied and extraordinarily complex (Rutter, 1986).

Diagnostic procedures are advocated that are chiefly descriptive in nature and take special cognizance of the syndrome, rather than symptom, nature of this disorder. Prevalence estimates vary enormously as a function of the specific criteria used to define depression. Rutter (1986), in his Isle of Wight study, reported that 40% of his sample of 14- and 15-year-olds experienced substantial feeling of misery and depression. Moreau (1990) noted estimates ranging from 0.14% to 49%, depending upon the measures and criteria used to define depression. Kashani et al. (1987) used *DSM-III* criteria in his epidemiological study to conclude that 4.7% of his sample of 14- to 16-year-olds suffered a major depression. Kutcher and Marton (1989) estimated a prevalence of about 2.6% for boys and 10.2% for girls in early to middle adolescence. A recent review by Hammen and Rudolph (1996) suggests rates of childhood depression between 6% to 8%, with those for younger children being lower than that of adolescents. They also note the interesting finding that rates of depression appear to be increasing.

The more carefully structured the diagnostic process, the lower the prevalence of depression. This is due to the fact that many items to which young people are asked to respond identify states of unhappiness that are transient and are not necessarily attributable to clinical depression. Investigators, such as Lewinsohn and Clarke (1990) and Stark (1990), routinely utilize structured interviews in addition to rating scales in order to obtain research samples whose depressions conform to *DSM* criteria. More experienced clinicians will observe that even when using stringent criteria, a diverse population of depressed individuals emerges in terms of symptom clusters, family functioning, and a host of other variables, to say nothing of the difficulties inherent in attempting to address the presumed etiological factors underlying the disorder.

This author advocates an assessment procedure that utilizes *DSM-IV* criteria for the establishment of a diagnosis of major depression. The literature emphasizes assessment of the young

19

person from multiple perspectives, including parents and schools, as well as through the use of structured interview formats (Carlson et al., 1987; Silverman, 1994). Economy, as well as the subjective nature of many symptoms of depression, dictates the use of depression rating scales. Carlson et al. (1987) speak to the difficulties in establishing "caseness" with child and adolescent disorders given the differing views that parents, teachers, and other children may have of the child. This is compounded in the case of depression by the subjective nature of so many of the disorder's symptoms. Nonetheless, Reich and Earls (1987) have suggested that adolescents are quite capable of reliably reporting internalizing disorders and that a diagnosis may be established based solely on the young person's report. Cantwell et al. (1997) recognize that practice economic and time constraints make it unlikely that practitioners will fully explore youth and parental perspectives. They also note that internalizing disorders of adolescence are more likely to be diagnosed just by youth interviews.

A vast array of rating scales for assessing adolescent psychopathology exists in the literature (Matson, 1989). Because of the likelihood that perhaps 40% of depressed adolescents meet the criteria for a comorbid disorder, assessment must not be so narrow as to focus only on depression. The perspectives of young people and their parents are often divergent; and therefore it is advocated that measures be employed for both points of view, and that they be broad-based enough to sample the entire spectrum of psychopathology. Perhaps the most widely used measure is the Child Behavior Checklist (CBCL; Achenbach & Edelbrock, 1983) which includes both parent and youth forms. In addition, the CBCL assesses both internalizing and externalizing disorders.

There are also numerous self-report rating scales of depression. Two scales are recommended for this age group (13 to 18): the Reynolds Adolescent Depression Scale (RADS; Reynolds, 1987) and the Beck Depression Inventory (BDI; Beck, 1978). Both scales come with companion scales that assess hopelessness and suicidality.

In mental health and behavioral health care settings, paper-and-pencil screening of new patients is strongly advocated as a method for determining which particular specialty clinic within an outpatient program is best able to complete the assessment process and initiate treatment of the young person and his or her family. In the case of depression, given the crisis nature of the presentation in some cases, as well as the possibility of suicidal ideation, long delays in scheduling are ill-advised. While some flexibility in data collection procedures may be necessary to meet the immediate needs of the patient, screening using the preceding measures is still well advised after immediate crisis issues are addressed.

The use of structured interview techniques is also advocated, such as the Diagnostic Interview for Children and Adolescents-Revised (DICA-R; Reich et al., 1982), and its *DSM-IV* version. The DICA-R is easily administered by personnel from a wide range of backgrounds and experience. It can be completed in 45 to 50 minutes and yields sufficient information to diagnose a variety of Axis I disorders. Forms exist for child, adolescent, and parent administrations. Separate interviews of the adolescent and parent(s) are advised.

Because of the familial nature of at least some affective disorders, as well as the likelihood of family problems, the use of rating scales dealing with parental, individual, and family functioning are also advocated. Examples include the SCL-90 (Derogatis, 1983) for parents and the Family Environment Scale (FES; R. H. Moos & B. S. Moos, 1984) to assess family conflict and overall family functioning.

Finally, while rating scales and structured interviews can provide adequate data to establish or rule out the presence of disorders in the individual young person and his or her parent(s), family interviewing, at least including the index patient and parent(s), is necessary to determine the complex nature of family issues.

SUMMARY

An assessment protocol is advocated that includes the following:

1. Psychopathology screening scales, which tap into both the youth's self-report and parental perceptions. The CBCL

is recommended because it is broad-based and includes forms for parents, youth, and school personnel.

2. Rating scales for self-reports of depression in youth, including the BDI and the RADS. The Reynolds companion scale for suicidal ideation is also recommended.

3. A review of school records and medical records is advised. School records include data on special education placements; individualized educational plans (IEPs); and past psychological, intellectual, and achievement tests. Information from the school may also provide considerable data regarding the young person's overall adaptive functioning. Similarly, medical and physical examination records may provide data regarding the presence of a medical disorder that may be inducing a current depressive disorder.

4. A parental rating scale, the SCL-90, should be employed to help guide the clinician in making treatment recommendations, possibly for the parent(s) should they require treatment.

5. The DICA-R should be employed as a structured interview, administered separately to the parent(s) and the young person, in order to establish the presence of *DSM-IV* major depression and comorbid disorders.

6. A family interview should be conducted following the data collection to review the data, to determine family-level disturbances, and to make specific treatment recommendations. Guidelines for a semi-structured interview to assess expressed emotion and family conflict are appended to Mueser and Glynn (1995).

7. It is recommended that the assessment protocol be employed flexibly, in accord with the needs of the individual young person and his or her family. For example, a new case presenting in suicidal crisis will require a much speedier and streamlined initial intervention. Similarly, a grief-stricken young person may require tactful interviewing on several occasions before using any formal paper-and-pencil measures. By the same token, while the DICA-R is designed to be administered in one 45- to 50-minute interview, flexibility is encouraged to address the needs of

each patient and the demands of each clinical situation. The clinician is encouraged to be similarly flexible in conducting family interviews depending upon the sensitivity and nature of the issues uncovered in the earlier assessment phase.

The clinician working with depressed youth must always be guided by the recognition that depression in young people is varied and multifaceted. Young persons meeting the diagnostic criteria for *DSM-IV* major depression may differ in their symptom configurations, severity indicators, and adaptive functioning (La-Bruzza, 1994). Similarly, the factors contributing to the development and maintenance of their difficulties, as reflected in their life histories and family functioning, will vary greatly. Nonetheless, fidelity to the basic assessment model outlined previously should provide the data needed to assess and treat depressed youth.

INDIVIDUAL TREATMENT OF ADOLESCENT DEPRESSION

EDUCATION AND SOCIALIZATION INTO TREATMENT MODEL

In this and the following sections, numerous clinical vignettes will be used to demonstrate applications of cognitive and problem-solving strategies. Case material has been selected that demonstrates successful implementation of these techniques. The vignettes are intended to be illustrative, without being glib about the difficulties of implementing these approaches. The author makes no bones about the fact that this approach has yet to be subjected to rigorous clinical trials. Experienced clinicians reading these vignettes will surely understand that vignettes of failed intervention could just as easily have been included. In all cases, the material has been disguised to preserve anonymity.

A key component of cognitive therapy (Beck et al., 1979), and indeed many briefer psychotherapies (Garfield, 1989), is an early effort to educate the patient about the treatment model and to socialize the patient to that model. In cognitive therapy, this takes the form of assigned readings (Beck & Greenberg, 1976) and "mini-lectures" regarding the nature of depression as well as the structure of cognitive therapy.

Once the young person has been assessed and is deemed appropriate for a trial of outpatient therapy, it is important to educate the young person regarding depression. A mini-lecture consists of perhaps a 5-minute talk given by the therapist regarding depression and its impact on thinking and mood. This process is facilitated by weaving in data from the patient's rating scales and structured interview. Young persons will often recognize depression as a state of sadness, but are less likely to recognize their irritability as a reflection of their depression. Young persons are also unlikely to recognize that their thinking has altered as a function of depression. In delivering a mini-lecture the therapist is well advised to incorporate the young person's self-report data. This data can be replayed in a manner that helps the young person recognize that seemingly disparate aspects of his or her daily functioning can be organized under the rubric of a major depression. It is also important to help the young person voice and dispel any faulty assumptions about his or her behavior.

Clinical Vignette

Therapist: So when we put all this together - I mean your recent temper, your hopelessness, the sleep problems, and losing interest in school and baseball - it adds up to what we call a major depression, John.

Patient: So you mean I'm not an asshole?

Therapist: What do you mean, John?

Patient: I've been so crabby, I even yelled at my coach Monday. I've never done that before. (Silently slumps deeper into chair.)

Therapist: No, it sounds like what I mean by depression, and it sure doesn't make you a bad guy. John, you said this crabbiness started only a few months ago, along with other problems. Since it's part of depression, I think

	it's treatable. How about you and I work on the crabbiness?
Patient:	Sure. Everybody I care about seems to be sick of me right now. I didn't know it had to do with depression, though.

Clinical experience suggests that adolescents are often initially reluctant to engage in "homework" assignments. Nonetheless, it is important for the therapist to socialize the young person into an action therapy as rapidly as possible, beginning with the educative phase. This may involve meeting twice weekly, and breaking the reading into sections. In the final assessment or first treatment session, an early assignment may be to read the *Coping With Depression* pamphlet (Beck & Greenberg, 1976), or Reinecke's (1992) adaptation for adolescents. A section on depression, appended to Mueser and Glynn (1995), may be useful reading for both adolescents and their families.

Flexibility is required when dealing with depressed young people for whom reading assignments may be linked to school difficulties, or authority conflicts. In such cases, exploration of homework-related issues may provide a gold mine of information regarding automatic thoughts or developing schematic material.

It is important for parents to be educated about the syndrome nature of the disorder. In the process of this educative phase, the therapist will often encounter important information regarding family interpretations of the depressed young person's behavior.

Clinical Vignette

Father:	She just sits on her ass all day. She's just lazy.
Mother:	Well, she hasn't always been that way. But, over the last 3 months or so. . . .
Father:	She just sits on her butt, watching TV.

The parents, especially the father, are negatively labeling as "lazy" behavior what is more productively seen as a symptom of major depression - chiefly anhedonia, hopelessness, or psychomotor retardation. It is important to remember that in dysthymia, the

25

overlap with oppositional defiant disorder (Rapoport & Ismond, 1990) may make it more difficult to sort out what may be behind "laziness." In the preceding case vignette, however, the parents, especially the mother, give evidence of the time-bound quality of the behavior and its covariation with other symptoms of major depression.

Clinical Vignette

Therapist: Mrs. Jones, you said Susan hasn't always been that way?

Mother: Yes. Only these past 3 months, or so.

Therapist: Since the crying spells and talk of hurting herself started?

Mother: Well, yes.

Therapist: Mr. Jones, how do you see this? Did Susan's lying around start about 3 months or so ago as you see it? Do you see it like your wife, or differently?

Father: Oh, I suppose she wasn't always this bad. Seems like it's gradually gotten worse, like Mary says.

Therapist: Would you say, Mr. Jones, that Susan is generally lazy?

Father: She's never been all that fired up about getting things done around home. But it's sure as hell gotten worse this spring.

Therapist: OK. Sounds to me like her lying around this spring might be due to depression. How about we talk more about depression and see how that fits with what you've been seeing in Susan these past few months?

As the preceding vignette demonstrates, family members may harshly and erroneously mislabel the behavior of the young person as something other than an emotional disorder. It is therefore important in major depression to help all members of the family correctly identify depression as the source of the problem, rather than global defects in the young person or his or her parent(s).

It may be of benefit for the therapist to meet with the young person and parent(s) together, in order to dispel the previous kinds of misperceptions. By doing so, the family's capacity for collaboration, joint problem solving, and restoration of trust may ensue.

Socializing the young person to the treatment model can be done through the use of handouts, through mini-lectures during initial therapy sessions, and by simply being guided by the therapist into a treatment routine. Mini-lectures should be relatively brief with adolescents. It is believed that the collaborative empiricism of cognitive therapy is well suited to developing a treatment relationship with adolescents, and can be employed to help young persons reach an initial understanding of the components of the treatment model.

The basic components of the treatment model, to which the adolescent should be socialized, include:

1. The structure of a typical therapy session:

    *   Review of issues from previous session
    *   Homework review
    *   Agenda setting
    *   Problem solving
    *   Homework assignments
    *   Review of session

2. The role of automatic thoughts in the production and/or maintenance of negative mood states.
3. Description and monitoring of mood states.
4. Situational aspects of moods and automatic thoughts.
5. Self-monitoring the relationship between thinking and mood states in daily life.
6. The use of therapeutic experiments to test out appraisals of problem situations.
7. The use of problem-solving techniques in the young person's specific life situations.

The socialization of the young person to the general format of a therapy session can occur as the therapist leads the young person through the initial sessions. Anchoring the relationship in an agreement to work on specific problems of concern to the young person also helps shape the young person to the contours of the treatment model. Individualization and flexibility are possible advantages of this model over other group-administered cognitive-behavioral treatments. Nonetheless, an effort must be made to essentially train or teach the young person how to maximize the benefits of psychotherapy.

Once a young person can recognize that he or she has a major depression, and that certain key life problems arise out of, or are worsened by, this disorder, it is easier to gain compliance with treatment procedures. For example, if a young person is troubled by his recent "blow ups" at a girlfriend, he is encouraged to recognize this behavior as a possible component of his depression. He can then be encouraged to target such episodes for intervention, including monitoring his mood and automatic thoughts in similar problematic situations.

The preceding procedure allows the therapist to gradually and systematically introduce key aspects of the treatment model over the course of the first two or three sessions.

Cognizance is taken of the varying capacities of adolescents to describe and monitor mood states. For example, young persons who have difficulties identifying mood states may require a variation of Stark's (1990) affective education program. However, most depressed young persons are acutely aware of negative mood states and may have a more difficult time tuning in to automatic thoughts. Techniques for dealing with this will be described later in this guide.

INDIVIDUAL TREATMENT TECHNIQUES

Cognitive Therapy Techniques. A difficult task for this age group is that of decentering, which Safran and Segal (1990) describe as "experiencing one's own role in constructing reality" (p. 6). This involves seeing one's own view of reality in nonabsolute terms, a difficult enough task for adolescents, made more difficult when depression invades the young person's thinking.

Young persons with difficulties decentering are prime candidates to be reached via problem-solving interventions. Helping the young person understand how depression encroaches upon thinking may remove the sting from learning that his or her thinking contains relativistic, nonabsolute components.

The use of the standard cognitive therapy approach of collaborative empiricism is particularly helpful in working with adolescents. Here is an example of how it can be used to help a young person decenter.

Clinical Vignette

Patient: I know nobody at home listens to me. It's no figment of my imagination. They never, never take anything I say seriously.

Therapist: Susie, you may be absolutely right about this. If you are right, and nobody ever listens, maybe we can find some ways to get them to listen better. Would you be willing to just test out this idea, as a beginning?

The therapist does not immediately challenge the young person's all-or-nothing thinking. Rather, acknowledgment is made of the possibly accurate nature of her perceptions, while gently enlisting her as a "co-investigator." It is important to frame such efforts as no-lose situations, so that being "wrong" is a source of mastery experience, rather than of humiliation.

Agenda Setting. Agenda setting is more difficult to establish with adolescents than adults. When good rapport is established between a young person and a therapist, the young person may wish to stray from structured problem-solving formats. This may represent a wish for the kind of mirroring and merger with the therapist that Elson and Kohut (1987) have described. It is important to allow opportunities for the young person to "update" the therapist and ventilate about events that have occurred since the previous session. However, it is not deemed helpful from the perspective of this treatment model to drift away from the basic structure of cognitive therapy sessions. This is not to compare the developmental stage of adolescence to adult Axis II disorders. Rather, it urges the therapist to recognize that the needs of the young person for mirroring, support, encouragement, and approval may at times be more important than a focus on the formal aspects of the cognitive therapy session. This may be particularly salient with young people whose parenting has been impaired due to parental psychopathology, marital conflict, death of a parent or sibling, divorce, or prolonged family stressors.

An example of how to incorporate these needs into an agenda-setting framework follows.

Clinical Vignette

Patient: I got cut from the cheerleading squad this week. (Cries.) Nobody understands how much this hurts. My mom and dad just blow it off and think I should just forget it, like it's not a big deal. I've been waiting since Monday to talk with you about it.

Therapist: I'm really sorry, Jan. I know how hard you worked to make the team. What hurts worse, thinking that Mom and Dad didn't understand, or just getting cut from the squad?

Patient: Both. But Mom and Dad's reaction really hurts, so much.

Therapist: What do you say we put that on our agenda for to-day's session? How about we look at what happened and see if we can find a way of looking at it that will help deal with the hurt.

In this vignette, the therapist acknowledges and attends to the hurtful event. The therapist is careful to avoid the trap of basking in the glow of the patient's idealizations. It can be especially tempting for therapists to derive undue pleasure from being more lovable to a young person than are the young person's parents. This occurs in the previous vignette when the patient says "I've been waiting since Monday to talk with you about it." From a cognitive and problem-solving perspective, the therapist wants to encourage a young person to develop and utilize healing resources available in the family of origin, rather than relying solely on the therapist. Boszormenyi-Nagy (1987), Boszormenyi-Nagy and

Krasner (1986), and Boszormenyi-Nagy and Spark (1973) write elegantly on this subject.

Picking items for the therapy agenda generally flows from the diagnostic phase as target symptoms, or clusters of symptoms, emerge for therapeutic intervention. Just as the patient is encouraged to establish agenda items for each session, the therapist has a responsibility for which issues are to be dealt with, and in what order. For example, if a young person is currently contemplating suicide, no therapist would allow the agenda to first include making a decision about trying out for the basketball team. A process of give and take, shaped by the therapist's familiarity with depression in young people, is necessary. However, the young person should be supported whenever possible in contributing issues for work in each therapy session.

Monitoring the Relationship. In this regard, a further component of cognitive therapy that can be helpful with adolescents is the frequent monitoring of the relationship between patient and therapist. As part of the process of establishing a collaborative relationship, patients are encouraged to verbalize their perceptions of the current therapy hour, as well as perceptions of the therapist. These perceptions may be scrutinized for their truthful as well as distorted qualities. It can be a very freeing experience for an adolescent to be able to state his or her perceptions of an adult in a way that allows for nonpunitive exploration of the basis for those beliefs. The therapist must be benevolent toward the young person, yet dispassionate regarding the young person's appraisal. The purpose of eliciting such perceptions is to deepen the collaborative relationship with the young person by inviting an open exchange regarding how the therapy is progressing, as seen through the eyes of both participants.

Clinical Vignette

Therapist: Any thoughts about our last meeting?
Patient: Well. . . .
Therapist: You looked a little upset when you left last time, and you've been pretty quiet so far today. Can you give me some idea of what's up?

Patient: Well, I was pretty angry when I left here last time.

Therapist: Oh yeah? Can you remember exactly what happened, or what I might have done or said that made you angry?

Patient: First, it was just the look on your face when I didn't do all of the homework. Like you were just disgusted with me, or something. I felt like such a jerk, and it made me mad that you were judging me like that.

Therapist: The look on my face, huh? Well, tell me, was there also something I said when I had that look on my face that also got you mad?

Patient: I don't remember. We sort of went on and talked about why I didn't get the homework done. I didn't bring in any today, either.

Therapist: Was this again because in some way you think I am judging you?

Patient: I just don't want to feel like a jerk. Like if I don't do it the way you want, I'll be some kind of jerk.

Therapist: I see. So you were already nervous about bringing in a homework assignment because you were afraid it wouldn't measure up. Then when you saw a look on my face, you really got upset.

Patient: Yeah, something like that. That's pretty much how it is.

Therapist: Well, you know, it sounds like something we've talked about before in a way. You told me stuff like that happens with other adults, like your teachers and folks.

Patient: Yeah. (Laughs.)

Therapist: OK. Look, I don't recall feeling or thinking such awful things about you during our last session. Can you show me the face I made last time?

Patient: (Scrunches up face into an angry scowl.)

Therapist: Really? Wow! That looks like an angry face. Sometimes I think I get a serious look on my face when I'm thinking. Do you suppose it's possible that I was being serious, rather than angry?

Patient: Yeah, I guess so.

Therapist: Tell you what. If you see that face again, will you let me know? It sounds to me like you'll figure I'm

>   judging you again unless you say something to me,
>   and get a sense of what I see going through my mind
>   at the time.
>
> *Patient:*   If you're really mad at me, will you tell me?
> *Therapist:* (Laughs.) It's a deal.

The therapist and patient replayed a common pattern in the patient's life: the belief that she would fail to meet the expectations of important adults in her life, and the tendency to interpret adults as angry with her for her perceived failures. Her increasing tendency to withdraw, perhaps passive-aggressively, from meeting task demands only exacerbated this interpersonal dilemma. By dealing with this in a forthright manner, the therapist encouraged the patient to test out her automatic thoughts immediately within the therapy session. Once this relationship issue and the automatic thoughts underlying it are dealt with, compliance with homework and other treatment processes is more likely to occur.

If the therapist were irritated with the patient, the obvious hazard exemplified in the previous vignette could be the possibility of attributing the patient's perceptions to distorted thinking. The therapist should always scrutinize his or her own internal experience for signs of anger or irritation with adolescent patients. Depressed young people, particularly with well-entrenched interpersonal problems, can indeed be difficult. Nonetheless, it remains the therapist's duty and responsibility to manage and contain negative affects, thoughts, and behaviors toward young people. Cognitive self-therapy for the therapist may be useful in maintaining a realistic and benevolent approach to young people (Burns, 1989). Based on experience in situations such as the preceding vignette, the therapist is well advised to acknowledge and deal with the situation as honestly as possible when the patient accurately perceives the therapist's thoughts and affects.

Self-Monitoring.   Ideally, self-monitoring homework can be assigned in the second session. Although the ultimate goal of self-monitoring will be a log (Burns, 1980, 1989) of automatic thoughts and moods in specific situations, it is always advisable to begin with a small, manageable assignment and build from there. A beginning assignment might consist of asking the young person to monitor the situations in which painful emotions occur. If a young person is reluctant to engage in written self-monitoring, some coaxing may be in order.

Clinical Vignette

Patient: I don't like the idea of writing this stuff down, I guess. It's too much like schoolwork. (Laughs.)

Therapist: Well, it is a kind of homework assignment, but you don't get a grade for it. Hopefully, it'll help us fix the problems we've been talking about. You said you're always angry and blow up at people.

Patient: Yeah. Then I feel terrible afterwards.

Therapist: So, how about we just start by seeing exactly when and how your temper gets uncorked. Then we'll work on some ways to change that.

If the young person appears unable or unwilling to engage in the kind of hourly and daily self-monitoring that is employed in cognitive therapy with adults, the therapist can start small. For example, if the patient is being asked to monitor a mood or situation that has a relatively high likelihood of occurrence, he or she can agree to note it on only one or two occasions between meetings.

Clinical Vignette

Therapist: So you don't think you'll actually write down the whole mood log?

Patient: Probably not, to be honest.

Therapist: OK. How much do you think you can handle, Don?

Patient: Maybe I can do it for one day.

Therapist: That'll be a good start. Which day do you want to do?

Patient: I don't know. Does it matter?

Therapist: Well, is there anything coming up this week where you think you might feel sad and think that you're a loser?

Patient: I'll probably see my ex-girlfriend tomorrow night at a party, and she'll probably be there with her new boy-friend. I could see what automatic thoughts I have then and write them down later. I'd feel pretty silly taking out a little notebook right there at the party.

Therapist: So you'll write those thoughts down later, along with a mood rating?

Patient: Sure. No problem.

Once a young person actually monitors for the presence of automatic thoughts, a large spectrum of techniques can be brought to bear on challenging those thoughts (Schrodt, 1992). Among the more helpful techniques for changing young persons' depressive appraisals are:

1. Examining the evidence.
2. Looking for alternative explanations.
3. Use of visual analog scales.

Examining the evidence is predicated on the use of an experi-mental model in which young persons are encouraged to treat automatic thoughts as hypotheses.

Clinical Vignette

Peter was a 16-year-old male who met the criteria for both dysthymia and major depression. The onset of his depres-sion coincided with the death of his mother when he was 10 years old. During the course of self-monitoring for automatic thoughts during especially sad periods, the thought "It was all my fault" was revealed. Peter stated that during the preceding week, he had become aware of that thought on several occasions when his mood had been especially low.

Therapist: Peter, what evidence do you have that your mom's death was your fault?

Patient: If I'd stopped her from driving that night she'd never have gotten in that wreck?

Therapist: So your evidence that your mom's death is your fault is. . . .

Patient: I should've stopped her from driving to work?

Therapist: She drove every night?

Patient: Yeah.

Therapist: I see. Peter, do you have a crystal ball?

Patient: Huh?

Therapist: Can you tell the future?

Patient: I wish. No.

Therapist: So how could you know she'd get in a wreck that night? I mean, what happened that told you that night would be any different?

Patient: I guess nothing. I just wish I could've known. (Cries.)

Therapist: So you could've warned her?

Patient: Yes.

Therapist: But, Peter, since you don't have a crystal ball, how could you have warned her? What would she have said if you'd said, "Mom don't go. You're going to get in a wreck and die tonight"?

Patient: She'd have said I was crazy, or worrying for nothing.

Therapist: I see. So even if you'd warned her, she wouldn't have listened.

Patient: No.

Therapist: So, if we look at all the evidence, how can this have been your fault?

Patient: I guess it really wasn't my fault. I just wish Mom were still here; but, I guess it isn't my fault she's not.

Some therapists rely on awareness generated during the therapy hour to transfer to everyday life. In contrast, cognitive therapy deliberately works to bring new awareness out of the therapy hour and into the patient's everyday life. In the preceding case, the young person might be encouraged to counter future thoughts, such as "Mom's death is all my fault," with more realistic self-statements generated during the therapy hour.

The general technique of examining evidence can be used with an enormous range of distorted thinking. As Schrodt (1992) observed, a young person's depressed thinking is not distorted, per se. Rather, an accurate recognition of a personal frailty, interpersonal hurt, or failure to accomplish a goal leads to a catastrophic inference. A young person who fails to make the football team as starting quarterback may conclude "My life is over. I'll never amount to anything." A girl who is rejected by a boyfriend may conclude "Now I'll be alone forever. No one will ever love me." The therapist must acknowledge the grief and pain inherent in these situations of loss or disappointment, and guide the young person to the awareness that setbacks are not proof of worthlessness or unlovability.

Wilkes and Rush (1988) note that looking for alternative explanations may in many cases prove more effective than examining the evidence. The simple question, "What's another way to look at it?" can help the young person consider more benign and possibly more accurate views of a problem situation. The therapist might also ask a young person to imagine how someone else in the problem situation might view that situation. The experimental method can be used to test out which of a variety of possibilities may be most accurate or useful.

Clinical Vignette

Therapist: Joe, you said you got furious with Sharon because she had to get off the phone last night. You also said you told yourself it meant she didn't love you anymore.

Patient: Yeah, that's what I thought.

Therapist: Is there some other way to look at what Sharon might have been thinking?

Patient: Well, I guess she could have thought that she'd better get off since her dad told her to. Maybe she just felt like she had to obey him. Actually, maybe that protected our phone time more than if she'd stood up to him.

Therapist: Which way of looking at it feels better to you?

Patient: The second way.
Therapist: Which way might be more correct?
Patient: (Smiling.) The second way.

Just as with adults, the use of a survey technique to test out inferences about various explanations can be employed. If the answer isn't clear from reviewing it in the session, the therapist could check with Sharon to find out what, in fact, she was thinking when she yielded to her father's command to get off the phone. If she states that she was afraid she'd have phone privileges revoked for 2 weeks, then Joe's alternative explanation is supported. If, on the other hand, she tells Joe that she really doesn't want to talk with him anymore, then opportunities exist to de-catastrophize Sharon's rejection of him.

Schrodt (1992) has observed that "Behavioral modification appears to be an essential component of sustained cognitive modification. 'Understanding' may lead to a change in mood, decreased helplessness, and increased engagement and participation in behavioral experiments. However, enduring change at the schemata level requires a change in behavior" (p. 209).

Perhaps the most commonly used behavioral method employed in cognitive therapy is activity scheduling. The use of an activity schedule (Burns, 1980, 1989) with young people can be employed both as a self-monitoring device and as a vehicle for longer-lasting behavioral change. Though much of a young person's day is, or should be, structured by school involvement, activity schedules can still be useful. For example, as a self-monitoring tool, activity schedules can be used to assess hourly or daily variations in mood, energy, or attentiveness in school. Problems maintaining acceptable activity levels after school and/or weekends can be addressed through the use of an activity schedule. The therapist working with young people must keep in mind the need for use of graded task assignments which may include gradually introducing more and more structure into the young person's life. As structure is added, the young person's predictions about the impact of structure are tested, challenged, and refined. Learning to counter a tendency to retreat, or yield to depressive lethargy, may provide a lifelong lesson on the importance of activity in mood regulation.

The Weekly Activity Schedule provided on pages 40-41 can be used in several ways. By breaking the day into hourly sections, interventions can be planned at strategically important times. For example, should the therapist and young person determine that mood drops frequently occur at specific times and days, those times can be targeted for intervention.

Similarly, well-established adaptive routines that have faded during a depressive episode can be reestablished using the activity schedule. For example, a young person may report difficulty getting out of bed in the morning, with a further drop in mood as he or she lays in bed, ruminating. The activity schedule can specifically target arising each day at a disignated time. Depending upon the sophistication of the young person, the activity can then be rated for the sense of mastery and pleasure that accompanies the completion of the targeted activities, such as getting out of bed, dressing, washing, and going to school. The completed activity schedule can then be used in the next session to validate changes in mood as a function of activity versus depressive rumination and withdrawal.

Visual analog scales have great utility in treating young people. They provide a simple means of assessing subjective levels of distress and the specific nature of mood states, as well as a measurement of change. Regardless of introspective capabilities or verbal expressiveness, young people almost always resonate to the idea of placing a mark on a line to show the therapist how sad they feel. Similarly, younger adolescents and preadolescents can fill in a circle with a face that describes their feeling states (see sample on page 45).

In the example on page 45, the use of a simple face drawing and a 0 to 100 scale are employed to assess both mood and the believability of a thought that co-occurs with depressed affect in a young person. Modifying a previous example slightly will demonstrate how visual analog scales and simple paper-and-pencil devices can be used in working with younger adolescents and preadolescents.

WEEKLY ACTIVITY SCHEDULE*

NOTE: Grade activities M for Mastery and P for Pleasure 0-10

	Monday	Tuesday	Wednesday	Thursday	Friday	Saturday	Sunday
6 a.m. – 7 a.m.							
7 a.m. – 8 a.m.							
8 a.m. – 9 a.m.							
9 a.m. – 10 a.m.							
10 a.m. – 11 a.m.							

11 a.m. - 12 p.m.	12 p.m. - 1 p.m.	1 p.m. - 2 p.m.	2 p.m. - 3 p.m.	3 p.m. - 4 p.m.	4 p.m. - 5 p.m.	5 p.m. - 6 p.m.

*Beck et al. (1979).

41

Clinical Vignette

James was a 12-year-old African-American male, whose mother had died 2 years before his being brought to treatment. The particulars of the case were such that his mother had sent him to the store with his cousin to purchase groceries. When he returned home, he found his mother on the floor of the bathroom, struggling to breath. He ran across the street to his grandparents home and they called 911. He returned to his mother's side, where he remained during efforts to resuscitate her. She was pronounced dead of a heart attack at the hospital. This young person initially showed signs of normal bereavement that abated within a year. However, nearly 2 years after his mother's death, he became severely depressed, showing signs of weight loss and sleep impairment, in addition to the affective and cognitive signs of major depression. His grandmother, with whom he now lived, brought him to the university hospital clinic for treatment. Because he met criteria for major depression, including vegetative symptoms, he was referred for both medication therapy, via a seratonin reuptake inhibitor, and cognitive therapy. He was seen for 10 sessions. The patient, James, described the following in the 7th psychotherapy session:

Therapist: Do you notice what kinds of things pass through your mind when you get that sad feeling you had at home this week? Maybe they are pictures, maybe thoughts.

Patient: I was thinking it was my fault Mom died.

Therapist: You mean that was what you noticed going through your mind this week when you were sad?

Patient: Yeah, I was thinking that it was my fault she died. (Begins to cry.)

Therapist: James, that really is a sad thought. Just thinking about it now even hurts me. Can you draw in a face that shows how you feel when that thought comes to mind? (James draws the sad face shown in Figure 1, p. 45.)

Therapist: James, I'm going to draw a little line here, that goes from 0 on one side to 100 on the other. I want to know just how much you believe that thought "It's my fault." In fact, I'll write that thought above the face, so we can look at how you feel when this thought is there. Now, can you put a mark on the line that shows just how much you believe that thought right now? (James places a dot on the line shown in Figure 1, p. 45, between 90 and 100, indicating that he strongly believes that his mother's death is his own fault.)

Therapist: You really do think it was your fault, don't you? James, what evidence do you have that shows you it was your fault Mom died?

Patient: Because I should have stayed at home with her instead of going to the store with my cousin.

Therapist: What a thought! James, could you write that under the "believability" scale on this page (see Figure 1, p. 45)? (James writes.) You mean you think you should have known, somehow, that Mom was going to die?

Patient: Yeah.

Therapist: James, had she been sick?

Patient: No.

Therapist: So how could you have known she'd die? Do you have a crystal ball, or anything else that lets you tell the future?

Patient: (Smiles slightly.) No I don't. But, if I'd been there, maybe I could've called 911, or got her some help sooner. And then she'd be alive.

Therapist: I'm not even sure that would've made a difference, James. But, the important thing is that you wish you could have known, and could have protected Mom somehow. Tell me something, James. Suppose you'd told Mom you weren't going to the store, because you knew she was going to have a heart attack and die while you were gone. What would she have said to you?

Patient: (Smiling.) She'd have whipped my butt.

Therapist: Really? She'd have whipped you?

Patient: No, but she'd have said "That's ridiculous," or something. And she'd have told me to just get to the store.

Therapist: So nothing you could have said would've mattered? Did you usually do what mom asked you to do? Did you usually obey her?

Patient: Yeah, I did what Mama told me to do.

Therapist: So, James, you would have needed a crystal ball to read the future. Then you'd have had to tell Mom you weren't going to follow her order to go to the store. And you said that you always obeyed Mom. And even if you disobeyed this one time, she wouldn't have believed you anyway. So what could you really have done, James?

Patient: (Silence.) Well, I guess I couldn't have done anything different.

Therapist: So was it really your fault? What do you think?

Patient: No. I don't think it could have been my fault, not really. It must've just been Mama's time to go.

Therapist: James, could you write that thought under the first thought (see Figure 1, p. 45)?

Patient: (Writes.)

Therapist: So how believable is that thought now? The one about Mom's death being your fault? (James first makes a star at 25%, then thinks for a moment and changes to 0%.)

Therapist: So what do you think? 25% or 0%?

Patient: Zero. It just couldn't have been my fault Mama died, could it?

Therapist: No, I don't think so, James. Will you take a copy of this sheet home with you? And if that sad thought pops back into your head, will you look at this sheet and remind yourself of what we did here?

In subsequent sessions, James reported that no further instances of depressive brooding occurred around this issue of personal responsibility for his mother's death. In fact, by the session that followed, James and his grandmother began to report improved sleep and appetite. James's mood improved, and remained brighter at 6-month follow-up after the completion of treatment. While James's improvement in mood may well have coincided with reaching a therapeutic level of antidepressant medication, his mood remained bright following discontinuation of the medication, and appeared to sharply coincide with the earlier therapy session. At the conclusion of this session, James was asked to show how he now felt by changing the picture, if he wanted. He drew a

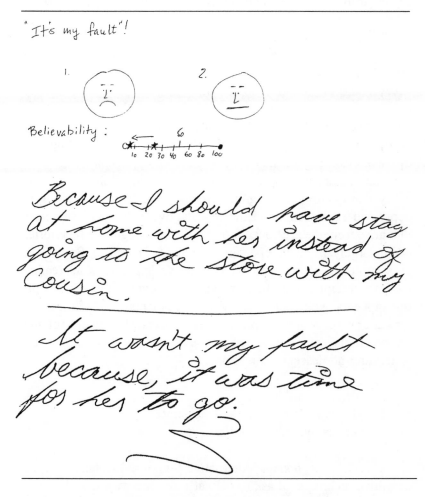

Figure 1. Using Visual Analog Scales.

second face, replacing the sad mouth with a more neutral straight line. He spoke with the therapist about not actually feeling "happy," since that would in some way imply a disregard for his mother's death. Most notable was the subjective lifting of depressed affect following the chance to openly talk about his depressive ideation and test it out for accuracy. Although this powerful therapy moment stands out, experienced therapists will recognize that many sessions do not proceed so smoothly, and many young persons require numerous sessions to be able to distance themselves from so powerful and damaging a belief as James harbored.

Problem-Solving Techniques. As previously noted, cognitive techniques alone may be insufficient for treating depression in this age group. Speculation regarding the poorly evolved capacity for decentering, or "thinking about thinking," was provided. A more concrete way to link cognitive and behavioral change is provided by the use of problem-solving strategies (D'Zurilla, 1988; A. M. Nezu et al., 1989; Spivack et al., 1976). It is worth noting that Spivack et al. regard their models as most applicable with interpersonal rather than impersonal problem-solving skills. It appears likely that even with a cognitive focus, distortions of thinking in depressed adolescents and the maladaptive behavioral strategies that arise from these erroneous and/or limited cognitive repertories occur largely in an interpersonal context. Therefore, Spivack et al.'s approach blends well with cognitive approaches in treating adolescent depression. Its somewhat less cognitively abstract format appears well suited to the developmental capabilities and limitations of young people. Three aspects of problem-solving interventions will be explored in this section for their application in treating adolescent depression:

1. Alternative thinking.
2. Means-ends problem-solving strategies.
3. Perspective-taking skills.

Alternative Thinking. Alternative thinking dovetails with the cognitive technique of asking "What's another way to look at it?" However, it involves systematically generating numerous options for solving a current problem situation. For depressed young people, the problem focus can range from their own thinking in a given situation to an exploration of alternative actions. It is necessary to briefly explore the general strategy used to generate alternative possibilities and then apply that strategy to two situations, using clinical vignettes.

Once a specific problem is identified by the therapist and the young person, the following steps are taken:

1. All possible options for alternative solutions to the problem are listed and written down.
2. The young person is encouraged to refrain from evaluating, negatively or positively, any option at this stage.
3. Alternatives from the list may be combined with other alternatives to generate new alternative solutions.

Remember that research on inhibited youngsters found them to be capable of generating the fewest alternative strategies of three groups studied (Spivack et al., 1976). This suggests the possibility, not yet researched, that depressed adolescents may be deficient in this crucial domain of adjustment, whether because of depression, or longer-standing cognitive deficits. The therapist should first encourage and, if need be, join the young person in generating alternatives.

Clinical Vignette

Sarah was a 16-year-old female whose boyfriend broke up with her. She was already depressed and the breakup precipitated suicidal ideation and a deepening sense of hopelessness.

Therapist: So you've become convinced that Harvey dumped you because you're a fat, unlovable pig?

Patient: Yes.

Therapist: Well, are you saying that you *are* a fat, unlovable pig, or are you saying that's how Harvey sees you?

Patient: He sees me that way, probably because I am.

47

Therapist: I see. So it's both, you and Harvey. OK, how about we just start with Harvey? One possibility is, as you're saying, that he thinks this of you. Let's write that down. Now, let's make a list of some other possible reasons for his dumping you.

Patient: There aren't any.

Therapist: Yep, there have to be others. Maybe not right, but there have to be others. Could be anything. Let's think.

Patient: Well, his dad's got cancer and maybe Harvey just can't think straight right now.

Therapist: OK, that's sure a possibility. Let's write it down. What else?

Patient: Maybe he has another girlfriend.

Therapist: Yeah. That could be, also. (Writes it on list.) You're doing great. Let's get as many possibilities as we can. Keep going.

Patient: This one is really silly. No, I can't even say it.

Therapist: Right now, let's just get as long a list as we can. We'll judge them later. Please, Sarah, put judgments away just for now. What were you thinking?

Patient: His parents are really religious. They've been pressuring him some to stay away from me. Maybe he's just doing what they want. (Writes it down.)

The likelihood is that Sarah's own appraisal of Harvey's reasons for dumping her is distorted. However, the therapist entertained that as one possibility, while encouraging her to generate other options. The therapist chose to focus on Harvey's motives, rather than Sarah's self-appraisal, because Sarah believed that without Harvey, life was not worth living, yet another depressive cognition. One of the real benefits of the preceding approach is that it helps foster a noncatastrophic, more benign outlook no matter which of the previous alternatives is most "true." For example, suppose Harvey indeed ended their relationship because he thought Sarah is a "fat pig." Sarah can then be helped to understand that perhaps Harvey has a problem and that now she is lucky to be rid of him. If she believes herself to be a fat pig, the whole spectrum of cognitive techniques can be used to help Sarah challenge this global, negative label.

Problem-solving approaches are more customarily applied to actions, rather than cognitions. Let us examine the application of generating alternative solutions to such a clinical situation.

<u>Clinical Vignette</u>

Sam was a 15-year-old male who saw another classmate, Eric, talking to his girlfriend, Sandi. Because Sam and his girlfriend had a volatile relationship, Sam feared that Eric was trying to steal Sandi from him. His first impulse was to simply punch Eric. After almost 10 sessions of therapy, Sam began to use a cognitive model to delay acting on his assumptions in similar situations. In the past, he had punched others and, on one occasion, broke three of his own fingers when he became angry and punched a wall.

Patient: I really want to punch Eric in the face. I know if I do I'm probably gonna feel like a total fool later, especially if he's really not that interested in Sandi.

Therapist: So, let's make a list of ways to handle this, and make it our goal to find some other ways besides punching Eric to deal with this.

Patient: How?

Therapist: Didn't you say you'll see Eric tomorrow morning in English class?

Patient: (Nods yes.)

Therapist: Well, what are some ways to deal with Eric tomorrow?

Patient: Well, what I want to do is hit him.

Therapist: OK. That's one possibility. What else?

Patient: I could ignore him, even if I see them talking. I could ask Sandi about it later, you know, like if she's getting interested in Eric. Eric and I used to be pretty good friends, so I could ask him. I'd feel silly doing that, though.

49

Therapist: Let's not evaluate any option yet, just come up with as many as we can.

Patient: I could ask another friend to tell Eric to lay off. I could dump Sandi today and just forget her, since she's not worth all this. I could try to trust what she told me last time something like this happened. (Laughs.) I could also break some more fingers hitting a wall, or something.

Means-Ends Thinking. This component of problem-solving involves critical evaluation of alternative strategies for achieving a goal, anticipating obstacles to the implementation of the strategy, and selecting one for implementation. Plans must be formulated to deal with potential obstacles that could materialize. Establishing a time perspective helps young people develop a greater capacity to delay impulse discharge and other immediate qualifications in the interest of achieving a goal of more enduring benefit to them. Once a strategy is selected, the young person and therapist determine a means of testing the strategy's effectiveness. It is important for a young person to understand that a perfectly sound goal-attainment strategy may require "mid-course corrections." Part of the therapist's work at this point involves helping the young person judge whether such a correction is necessary, and to design such a correction. Further testing and necessary modifications ensue until a goal is attained. This procedure merges with the collaborative empiricism of cognitive therapy. The systematic, concrete nature of this problem-solving approach enhances treatment effectiveness with depressed adolescents.

<u>Clinical Vignette</u>

(Strategy selection with previous case vignette continued.)

Therapist: OK, Sam, here's the list of alternatives we came up with:

1. Your first choice is to punch Eric.

2. Talk with Eric and Sandi.
3. Talk with Eric.
4. Ask a friend to meet with Eric.
5. Dump Sandi.
6. Trust Sandi.

Let's start with your first choice. What are the pros and cons of just punching Eric?

(The therapist can employ a cost-benefit analysis as outlined by Burns [1989].)

Patient: I'll feel great at first.
Therapist: Then?
Patient: I'll feel like a jerk. Sandi will be mad at me. I'll get suspended from school. The police might get involved, especially if I hurt him. Also, I basically think Eric is OK, so I'll feel really bad if I hit him.
Therapist: So, how would you evaluate hitting him then?
Patient: Advantages, about 10%, just because it'd feel good at the time. Disadvantages, about 90%. It's funny how the first thing I want to do is probably the worst one out of all the alternatives.

The therapist and Sam go through each of the alternatives until Sam can rank order them, and select the alternative most likely to help him achieve the goal of managing his anger and jealousy.

An example of implementing a means-ends problem-solving strategy follows:

Clinical Vignette

Miles was a 13-year-old boy suffering from major depression. He had shown features of anhedonia, and had increasingly withdrawn from previously pleasurable activities. One activity that he said he would have liked to resume was riding his bicycle with friends in the neighborhood. He stated that he believed that his grandparents, with whom he lived, wouldn't allow him to ride because they were angry with him because his grades had declined. While a family intervention could have been employed, the therapist elected to work with Miles individually. Miles's goal was to resume bike riding and he believed that his grandparents were an obstacle to that goal. After generating a list of alternatives, ranging from running away, giving up, or speaking to his grandparents, he chose to try the latter.

Therapist: So, you'll talk with them and see if it's OK to ride?
Patient: Yeah. I think that's the best thing to do. But I don't think they'll let me ride.
Therapist: That's a possibility, I guess. How about we find out?
Patient: OK. I'll try.

The therapist and Miles carefully planned how, when, and where to speak with his grandparents about bike riding. Then, the therapist asked Miles to imagine any obstacles that could have emerged. Miles identified what he believed was the most likely obstacle.

Patient: Grandpa will say no, because he's mad about my last report card.
Therapist: So, if you ask and he says no, what can you do? Let's plan something.
Patient: I could ask why, and when he says it's because of my grades, I would tell him my grades were bad this quarter because I was depressed. My grades are better now, and I deserve a chance to ride.
Therapist: Great. I like the way you're planning, Miles. Now, suppose Grandpa says no. What'll you do?
Patient: I'll say, "Grandpa, then what do I have to do to ride?" And, if he says "Get your grades up," I don't know, because I don't want to wait 9 weeks. What do you think I should do?

Therapist: Well, you could either ask if you have to wait until your next grade card, or you could show him homework assignments. We could also have a family meeting.

Patient: But, like we said, I want to try on my own first. If that happens, I'll say, "Grandpa, tell me what I've got to do to ride." I'll get it really clear, and if I have to wait, I'll wait. I think we'll work something out, though.

The patient returned the following session to report that he had spoken to his grandparents, who happily consented for him to ride. He noted that his grandfather told him he hadn't even needed to ask. This set the stage to not only review and provide praise for successful problem solving, but also to deal with the fact that his own appraisal had been skewed by his depression.

Perspective-Taking Skills. Perspective-taking skills involve helping a young person to not only understand "What's another way of looking at it?" as is done in cognitive therapy, but also, "How do others in this problem situation with you look at it?" This bears common features to the Survey Technique (Burns, 1989). A systematic effort to develop accurate appraisals of how others in a problem situation view that situation is encouraged. Not only can this help clear away depressively induced cognitive distortions, but it can lead to significantly better social problem-solving skills, as well. It was previously noted that Chandler (1973) utilized role playing as a means of developing empathy in conduct-disordered boys. Although a similar application to depressed adolescents has not been developed, such an application appears warranted. It is important to remain aware that not all of a depressed young person's interpersonal appraisals are likely to be distorted. For example, a depressed youth may behave in an aversive enough manner to truly alienate others and this must be dealt with in a forthright, direct, problem-solving manner.

Clinical Vignette

Sarah, the 16-year-old girl whose boyfriend, Harvey, broke up with her, reported in a subsequent session being very angry with her parents for expressing relief that she and Harvey had broken up. She had a stormy argument with them the night before the session.

Patient: They just hate me. They knew I was happy and they couldn't stand it.

The therapist could have relied on a "What's the evidence?" approach to deal with Sarah's perceptions. Another tactic is to simply and concretely encourage perspective-taking skills to be utilized or developed. This skill relates in some ways to the young person's capacity to develop other ways of viewing a situation. In this instance, the focus is on changing a stereotypical depressive view of others. The therapist's hope is to encourage a more flexible capacity to consider the experience and viewpoint of others. The therapist decides to guide Sarah into using the perspective-taking skills that have been eroded by her major depression.

Therapist: Sounds like we should put that on our agenda today. What do you think?
Patient: What good is it going to do? No matter what, they just don't want to see me be happy.
Therapist: Hmm. Could be. But, what do you say we take a look at last night's fight?
Patient: OK.
Therapist: You were telling yourself then that Mom and Dad can't stand to see you happy?
Patient: Yes.
Therapist: Can you put yourself right back there at home again, like playing a movie in your mind? (Patient closes eyes spontaneously.) At what point did you tell yourself that?

Patient: I was crying about Harvey and Dad came in and said, "He was a jerk. You're better off without him."

Therapist: And then?

Patient: I just went off. I started crying harder and yelling. It was awful.

Therapist: OK. So Dad said, "He's a jerk and you're better off without him." And what went through your mind was, "Dad just doesn't want me to be happy."

Patient: From my point of view, I don't know what Dad was thinking then.

Therapist: Maybe he just doesn't want you to be happy, like you say. Let me ask you to do something, though. Imagine for a minute being Dad right then. What did he see when he first came in?

Patient: Me crying.

Therapist: Do you think that made him happy? What do you think he could have felt when he walked in and saw you crying?

Patient: (Silence.) Sad for me. Angry at Harvey for hurting me, I guess.

Therapist: I see. Would you say you and Harvey were happy or miserable?

Patient: Pretty miserable, especially the last couple of months.

Therapist: So, if Dad wanted you to be unhappy, would he have wanted you to stay together, or split up?

Patient: (Laughs.) Stay together. That sounds silly when you put it that way.

Therapist: Let's look through Dad's eyes again. Has he known how miserable you've been?

Patient: Sure. Plus he found out about me and Harvey having sex.

Therapist: How might a dad feel about that?

Patient: Scared, angry. Probably worried.

Therapist: OK. So, if you just look at this situation through Dad's eyes, what do you see?

Patient: I'd be really worried that my daughter was going to get pregnant, and by a guy I think is a jerk.

The Use of Therapeutic Certificates. Certificates of accomplishment and/or graduation have been advocated by various therapists for work with young people, although none have written more elegantly on the topic than Michael White (White & Epston, 1990). Where appropriate, the therapist is encouraged to use his or her creativity to prepare a farewell certificate summarizing the accomplishments of therapy and commending the young person for their hard won therapeutic gains. Such certificates often provide a delightful reminder that can be looked over at future times, or shared with others in the family. Finally, therapeutic certificates cement a bond between therapist and young person that may help encourage the young person to return to treatment in the event of relapse into another major depression. An example of the use of such certificates follows, using the case of an inner-city adolescent, who met criteria for major depression and bereavement at the start of therapy.

Clinical Vignette

Donald was a 15-year-old African-American male, whose father had been murdered several months prior to his first session. Donald was described by family members as respectful and decent. He lived with his paternal grandparents, but had frequent contact with his father prior to his death. Donald's mother had died when he was quite young and his grandmother had mothered him. The family sought treatment because they were worried about how he might cope with his father's murder.

Donald was openly reluctant to speak during the first meeting. When asked why he had agreed to come in, he said, "My grandmama wanted me to, and I don't disrespect my grandmama." The therapist informed Donald that further sessions would be purely voluntary and stated he would so inform the family. The therapist also commended Donald for his respect of his grandmother, and wondered whether he might have comparable respect for his murdered father.

The story of this young person's anguished closeness with his episodically involved father followed. Donald was aware that his father had gone to an area liquor store where an unknown assailant shot him as he was leaving. No further details were known. Donald had roamed the streets looking for anyone who might know what had happened until his grandmother and grandfather persuaded him to stop. It occurred to Donald that he had no idea who had actually killed his father. However, because of his own strong physical resemblance to his father, he feared the assailant might harm him.

The murder occurred late in the summer, and Donald's serious problems did not emerge until the beginning of the school year. At that time, teachers reported that he had become uncharacteristically disrespectful. They observed that he did not stay in his seat, choosing instead to wander the rooms and/or halls of the building. His concentration and attention were unusually scattered, despite the continuing use of psychostimulant medications since he was a young boy. Finally, Donald's grandmother noted that the only thing he focused on was his basketball jumpshot, usually from the high school three-point range. She said that he spent hours daily perfecting his shot. Donald had played freshman basketball and was now in danger of academic ineligibility because of the school problems that occurred after his father's murder.

Five therapy sessions took place over a 2½-month period. Donald spoke lovingly about the one-on-one basketball games he had played against his late father. He indicated that he had become preoccupied with playing in the NBA, which would have made his father proud of him. He said that his father had once told him that he had the talent to play professional ball, and Donald wanted to do so to honor his father's memory. Initially, therapy placed these desires in the context of his school problems, and Donald was able to recognize that his first goal was to be able to play on the sophomore team. Then Donald was helped to examine whether the NBA was essential to secure his father's pride. Donald stated that he knew that

57

just graduating from high school and playing ball there would have made his father deeply proud of him.

The family was encouraged to speak to the basketball coach, who provided additional school-based guidance to Donald; and by session five, Donald, his grandparents, and an involved aunt and uncle reported that he was back in classes.

The sample therapeutic certificate on page 59 was sent at the conclusion of therapy, with the understanding that Donald was free to return as needed. In the final paragraph of the certificate, it stated that "Donald has healed up from the worst of his grief, at this time," to emphasize that at some subsequent time Donald may wish or need further sessions.

FAMILY THERAPY

Family therapy interventions will center around the following issues.

1. Family issues impacting on depression in the index patient. Other issues, such as those for which the marital dyad is the principal treatment focus, are not targets for intervention in treating the adolescent, and may require an outside referral.
2. Educative involvement of families is to be employed to better help families identify and correctly label the young person's behavior as evidence of depression.
3. Cognitive interventions adaptable to work with adolescents and the parent(s) will be used.
4. Problem-solving techniques will be utilized to engage families in collaborating with the adolescent to address issues relevant to the development and/or maintenance of the adolescent's depression.
5. Communication skills training will be used on an as-needed basis to enhance educative, cognitive, and problem-solving interventions.

SAMPLE CERTIFICATE OF
GRADUATION FROM THERAPY

This is to certify that Donald R. has worked hard to make sense of his life and of the murder of his father. Donald loved his father very, very much. In fact, he loved his father so much that he believed the only way to show his love was to make it to the NBA. He even quit working in school, and spent his time perfecting his jump shots when he was home. He started getting in trouble at school and at home. Nobody but Donald knew how much he was thinking about his father, and about how he wanted to honor his father's memory by being the "perfect" basketball player.

Donald realized that even though his dad loved to watch him play basketball, he would be especially proud if Donald graduates from high school. Once Donald realized that high school graduation would make Dad proud, just as much as an NBA contract, Donald lightened up a little on the practice and got back to the books. He still remembers those great one-on-one games with his dad. Donald knows he'll still get very sad sometimes when he thinks of those games with Dad, and realizes they're over for good. But, he'll be thinking of how proud Dad would be on graduation day, and he'll still be nailing down some three-pointers on the sophomore team.

That said, Donald has healed up from the worst of his grief, at this time, and deserves to be commended for the courage and decency he has shown in coping with his father's murder. He also deserves a special commendation for being the respectful and kind-hearted grandson that he is.

Signed this 1st day of June, 1995 .

Scott Temple, PhD
Scott Temple, PhD

6. Criteria for using family interventions include:

- The presence of specific interpersonal problems within the family that impact upon the index patient's depression. These issues are likely to be a blend of family and individual developmental issues, as well as psychopathology.
- Either the young person, the parent(s), or the therapist is free to identify such concerns, although it may be the therapist's responsibility to see that such issues are placed on the agenda and dealt with in therapeutic sessions. The kinds of issues that may be raised by young people and/or their parent(s) are negotiations regarding curfew, driving privileges, choice of friends, chores around the home, and allowances. Such issues are made a bit more complicated when intertwined with depression. For example, renegotiating friends and curfew following a suicide attempt is an added complication.
- While the young person's depression may range from moderate to severe, family dysfunction must be within the parameters outlined previously.

Family involvement is thus intended to be circumscribed with a clear focus on depression in the index patient. Nonetheless, preserving a nonblaming attitude toward family members serves to shore up others in the family who may be affected by the youth's depression.

COMMUNICATION TRAINING

Depressed young people in families with high rates of negative expressed emotion are thought to be at higher risk for future depressive episodes. At the very least, maintenance of depression is more likely in such families. Until family members learn to listen and speak to one another in less harmful ways, the effectiveness of cognitive and problem-solving strategies will be limited.

The following principles are advocated for use with families of depressed young people:

1. The therapist must remain vigilant to the presence of negative interchanges and must determine if such interchanges are characteristic of family functioning, or are limited to episodes of youth depression in the family.
2. The therapist must discourage the expression of negative interchanges, such as blaming, name-calling, yelling, and hostile nonverbal behaviors.
3. The therapist is more likely to accomplish this blocking of negative interchange when proper psychoeducational interventions have been implemented. The therapist must also intervene in a manner which communicates respect for all family members, even when they are engaged in destructive behavior.
4. Experience suggests that appeals to family members are more likely to succeed when accompanied by acknowledgments of caring. For example, "Mr. Jones, I know how much you are trying to keep Todd from making some of the mistakes in life that you believe you made. You're only looking out for his best interests. But, I notice that every time you point your finger and bark, he seems to turn off from you completely. I'd sure like to help you get across the message I know you want Todd to hear."
5. In families that appear stuck in long-term patterns of negative expressed emotion, an entire therapy component of communication skills training is indicated (Mueser & Glynn, 1995). However, it is quite often the major depression and the misunderstanding of that depression by family members that produces distortions in communication patterns. When psychoeducational and cognitive management interventions succeed, families can quickly move to problem-solving training.

COGNITIVE INTERVENTION

Just as the depressed young person is prone to distorted thinking, so too are family members prone to misappraisals of the depressed young person's inner state, motivations, and intentions toward family members. These attributions are targets for intervention at a family level. During the assessment process, the therapist should be alert for indications that the family is employing cognitive distortions in appraising the index patient. This is not to suggest that exasperation by parents of depressed young people is unwarranted. Exasperation does not necessarily reflect individual or family disturbance. However, families who mislabel the index patient's behavior, inner states, and intentions through such mechanisms as labeling, all-or-nothing thinking, mind-reading, and fortune telling, are likely to perpetuate the adolescent's problems. Such thinking, while not necessarily causally related to depression, should be seen as maintaining the depression of the index patient. Cognitive interventions that target such distorted thinking should be implemented when discovered in families.

Clinical Vignette

Jamie was a 14-year-old male who had become increasingly irritable during the previous 4 months. His grades had dropped, and he had retreated to his bedroom for longer and longer periods of time. Conflicts with his parents centered on his "attitude" and his noncompliance with doing chores. Jamie and his family had gone through a psychoeducational intervention about the nature of major depression and had some knowledge about depression, as well as the treatment approach in the clinic.

Patient: (To parents.) Nothing I do is ever right as far as you guys are concerned.

Therapist: Can you think of an example?

Patient: Yeah. I cut the grass yesterday, and left about five blades around a tree in back and Dad was all over me.

Therapist: So, that meant Dad didn't notice all the other blades you *did* cut?

Patient: Not as far as I can tell.

Therapist: OK. Let's find out. Ask Dad what he noticed. Let's see if he thinks you did any of it right.

Patient: (To father.) Well, I still get the idea that you don't think I do anything right.

Father: You know, Jamie, sitting here now, I guess I don't pay enough attention to stuff you do.

Mother: Dad always looks for the little things that you don't do right, all the little details, I think.

Father: Actually, though, I did notice how you put in the railroad ties for the flower bed. It's really beautiful, Jamie.

Patient: You never said anything, and that was last week.

Father: I think it's like the doctor said before, I need to let you know. Otherwise, I can see how you'd just be left thinking that you never do anything right in my eyes.

Therapist: Jamie, what do you think now about this idea that Dad doesn't think you do anything right?

Patient: I guess he notices more than I thought, but doesn't say anything to me about what goes right - just my mistakes.

Therapist: I feel a homework assignment coming on. (Family laughs.)

In another case vignette, the therapist encourages the young person to test out, experimentally, a hypothesis. In this case the hypothesis, or automatic thought, is "They never listen to anything I say."

Clinical Vignette

Therapist: Jamie, Mom and Dad have been giving some ideas of things they'd like to see change in the family. Now's your chance.

Patient: What's the use, they never listen to anything I say, anyway.

Therapist: Hmm . . . Could be. Still, let's take a crack at it. If they would listen, what would you tell them you want?

Patient: (No eye contact with parents.) I want to see Sammy (a friend with whom Jamie recently got into trouble).

Therapist: Look at your folks. How about Mom? Look at Mom and tell her you want to be able to spend some time with Sammy.

Patient: Sammy's a nice kid. I'd like to be able to talk on the phone or have him over. (Subdued, hesitant voice.)

Mother: That boy's caused nothing but trouble. We both think he's bad news. (Nudges father, who nods.)

Patient: But I'm 15. I should be able to pick my friends. He's a good guy anyway. (Looks at therapist.) I told you.

Therapist: (Laughs.) Hold on, we've still got some work to do. Let's find out what Mom thinks will happen if you see or talk to Sammy. Ask her.

Patient: What do you think?

Mother: I'm afraid you'll skip school again.

Patient: Even from talking on the phone?

Mother: Well, probably not from that. What do you think, Merle? (To father.)

Father: I don't like Sammy, either. That's why we grounded you from talking to him or seeing him.

Patient: Even a 15-minute call?

Mother: Well. . . .

Therapist: Want to try an experiment? Jamie, Mom and Dad said you've been spending too much time lying around, and that you're not doing things that used to be fun, or the jobs at home that you used to do. If you're willing to resume some things, let's see if Mom and Dad will give something back.

Patient: They won't.

Therapist: Let's try.

Patient: I'll do my jobs at home this week. I'll feel a little better, and I know stuff needs to get done. Can I at least talk to Sammy on the phone?

Mother: Well. . . .

Therapist: Let's try one 15-minute call. If he skips school the next day, we'll know for sure they're bad news together. If not. . . . (Parents look at each other.)

Father: I'm game.
Mother: OK.

The therapist then firms up the ground rules of the "experiment," which is to test the parents' assumptions as much as Jamie's assumption. In the preceding vignette, Jamie sees that he is capable of impacting his parents' assumptions and behaviors with the therapist's help. If all goes well, Jamie is in a stronger position to ask for a resumption of privileges in the next session. Jamie has the opportunity to increase his own sense of efficacy in dealing with his parents, and parents and child are enabled to alter limiting beliefs that underlie their interaction patterns. The therapist models another crucial feature of this approach to therapy: large problems must be broken down into small, manageable parts. Patients must build from small successes, creating a model for changing their thinking and for solving life problems.

In the previous two vignettes, cognitive interventions, as well as the "experimental method," were demonstrated. It is now important to turn to problem-solving techniques to see how they can be applied to depressed young people and their families.

PROBLEM-SOLVING INTERVENTIONS

Problem-solving techniques detailed earlier in this guide are adaptable for work with families. These areas include:

1. Generating alternative solutions.
2. Means-ends thinking.
3. Perspective-taking skills training.

The author believes there are numerous advantages to beginning problem-solving work with perspective-taking skills training. In many conflict-laden families, a missing element may be the capacity to understand the viewpoint of others in the family. This may be particularly true where major depression occurs. For example, studies of marital dyads where one partner is depressed demonstrate higher conflict in the marriage (Beach, Sandeen, & O'Leary, 1990; Biglan et al., 1985). It is thought that depressed adolescents are similarly likely to be involved in a more conflictual interpersonal network. The depressive ideation that characterizes depression in young people lends itself to rigid, all-or-nothing interpretations of others. In addition, it is the nature of depression to produce relatively bleak views of one's social environment. Depressed young people, in sum, can be difficult for their families to deal with or understand.

At the same time, parental or family-wide issues may also impinge on the functioning of the young person, thereby amplifying conflict. When that occurs, it is not likely to be sufficient to just treat the young person's depression in isolation from working with family members.

On a deeper level, developing better perspective-taking skills can lead to a restoration of self-healing properties within the family. Such efforts have been labeled as "rejunctive" by Boszormenyi-Nagy (Boszormenyi-Nagy & Spark, 1973; VanHeusden & Van Den Eerenbeemt, 1987).

Clinical Vignette

Jim was a 16-year-old male who got drunk and was arrested for reckless driving following a "blow up" with his father. He also met criteria for major depression, with a history of two prior episodes, and with generally adequate baseline functioning between episodes. The session included father and son.

Therapist: So Jim, can you tell Dad what he did that got you so mad that night? Dad, let's you and I listen for right now, OK?

Patient: You're always yelling at me for something. I never do anything right as far as you're concerned.

Therapist: Oops. How about we stick just with that night. Jim, tell Dad about only that night. Always is too big a chunk to bite off right now.

Patient: I got home from work and you said I couldn't take the car. You were being deliberately mean to me.

(The therapist could elect to use cognitive approaches here, as Jim's statements suggest "mind-reading." However, the therapist elected to work on perspective-taking skills, instead.)

Therapist: Dad, do you recall not letting Jim drive that night?

Dad: Yes. He had been talking about driving into a bridge or telephone pole, and I. . . . (Voice drops, and becomes tearful.)

Therapist: Dad, can you get across in some way to Jim what it's like to be a dad who's scared his son'll kill himself if he goes out?

Patient: But I. . . .

Therapist: Jim, let's just give Dad a chance here. Are you willing to just see his viewpoint for a second, here? Then we'll get back to working out driving privileges. Dad, go ahead.

Dad: Jimmy, I was so scared, and so angry that I guess I just blew up. Mom and I helped pay for that car for you, and I couldn't stand the thought of letting you go out and hurt yourself like that. I wasn't trying to be mean. I just didn't want you to die, and that's what I was afraid of.

Patient: (Slumps in chair, avoiding eye contact with Dad.) I didn't look at it that way. I thought you were just trying to give me a hard time.

The development of perspective-taking skills need not always be accompanied by strong affect. Abreaction is not a goal when utilizing this intervention. Ultimately, establishing a more cooperative climate for solving the daily problems of living within the family is the therapeutic goal. An acknowledgment and awareness of the positions and needs of others in the family facilitates such problem solving.

Clinical Vignette

Teresa was a 15-year-old from a Hispanic family. Her father had two jobs, and was rarely available to the family

67

except on Sundays. He had suffered a heart attack 2 years ago. Since then, Teresa's mother had decided to get job training and go to work in order to relieve some of the financial burden on her husband. The couple had four children, with Teresa being the oldest. Teresa was implicitly expected to assume greater responsibilities for her siblings once her mother started working. These demands were coupled with her entry into high school and her own anxieties about school performance.

Therapist: So you had all of this going on at the same time, Teresa? Wow. Can you tell your mom how you see carrying so many burdens? What has this been like for you?

Patient: (To mother.) I know why you had to go back to work. But, I just feel like I can't handle everything I need to do in school and also do all the things you used to do when you were home. I tried taking care of my brothers and sisters, and getting some dinner ready every night. I just kept doing a lousy job of everything I tried to do. The harder I worked, the worse I did at everything.

Therapist: So, Mom, can you tell Teresa what you are hearing from her?

Mother: That maybe Dad and I are asking too much of you. Maybe we need to find some other ways of getting organized. Teresa, right now I just don't know what we'll do. For right now, Daddy and I both need to be working. I know you don't think you did too good, but Daddy and I are really proud of you.

Patient: But I blew it.

Mother: No, no. You got really depressed. I think I maybe blew it, but I just don't know what else we can do to make this work right now.

Therapist: Well, that sounds like a good problem for us to work on together. Tell me something, you two. Who else is in the picture that might be able to help out? Other family? Friends? Do you know other families in the same boat? How do they deal with this situation?

Mother and daughter engaged in understanding one another's viewpoint about a common problem situation. The therapist adopted the stance that each point of view was valid. In the process, cognitive distortions were also addressed, as Teresa conveyed her sense of failure, and of having let down her mother. The mother's empathic response, based on careful listening, cleared the way for a more matter-of-fact process for generating alternative solutions to the problem. That process began when the therapist speculated about possible ways other families in similar situations might handle the issue. The therapist also began speculating about available resources, beyond the nuclear family, for helping the adolescent.

The next session included the entire family: Teresa, Anita (13), José (11), Reuben (8), Mom, and Dad:

Therapist: Let's list all the ways anyone in the family can think of to solve this problem of getting these jobs done that Mom used to do. We're talking about from 3 o'clock, when you all start getting home from school, until 5:30, when Mom gets home.

José: We could hire a butler. (The whole family laughs.)

Therapist: OK, I've got a pad of paper here. Anita, could you help me by writing down all these ideas. Let's start with José's.

Anita: (Writing.) B-u-t-l-e-r.

Mother: We could ask my sister to come over maybe 2 days a week, just to help get things organized until things are running more smoothly.

Father: I think Anita could do more to help out. She's old enough. It shouldn't all be on Teresa's shoulders. Anita, you're not writing that one down. (Family laughs again.)

Therapist: Teresa, let's get your thoughts here.

Patient: I feel like I should do everything, but I just can't.

Therapist: How did it work when you tried to do it all?

Patient: I blew it. No, I guess I just couldn't do it all, especially when I got really depressed.

Therapist: OK, so we don't need to write that one down. It was already tried, and it didn't work out. Let's try some new ideas here. Who can help you out next time?

Patient: Anita could do more to help.

Therapist: Good. Let's write down some of those things she could do.

Consistent with the use of problem-solving techniques in individualized therapy, the entire family or subgroups of the family generate a list of possible alternatives. The family is also encouraged to generate the list without initially evaluating any alternative. Thus, in this example, even one child's wish for a butler was included in the list.

Once compiled, the family is taken through a process of evaluating the alternatives and collectively deciding on the merits of each. The therapist may support boundaries within the family by encouraging subsystems within the family to make and implement final decisions. The siblings might be encouraged to work out appropriate jobs each will do until the mother comes home. During this part of the session, the parents might be encouraged just to sit back and listen as their children solve the problem among themselves. Similarly, if one alternative is to invite the help of an aunt, the parents might discuss the merits of this and decide on a strategy for requesting help while the children listen.

Means-ends thinking is encouraged in the family by exploring ways of achieving the agreed-upon objective. Specifically, family members are encouraged to consider possible barriers to successful task completion, and to plan ways to overcome them. In addition, family members should have clear, agreed-upon criteria regarding what constitutes a successful outcome.

Particularly helpful to the family is the opportunity to collectively evaluate the merits of each of the alternatives they generated, and to rank order them. This constitutes a relatively structured family task whose mission is to bolster family cohesion and simultaneously solve a practical, definable problem.

In the last vignette presented, each option was explored, even the relative merits of hiring a butler. The family agreed upon two alternatives they would choose: first, the children were to define age-appropriate tasks they would assume in Mom's absence; and second, the parents would request that an aunt look in on the children at least twice a week until all were convinced that the family had successfully adapted to the mother's new work status. The children divided work chores, wrote down the list of chores and who would perform each chore, and agreed that their parents would monitor their completion. In that way, parental authority was present even when the parents were not physically present. At the same time, Teresa was supported in her supervisory role as the oldest child, while limiting her involvement to well-defined tasks.

In the following vignette, the family anticipates possible barriers to successful task completion and works toward dealing with them before they occur:

Clinical Vignette

Patient: If Aunt Vicky comes over, she's going to start telling all of us what to do, even if we've already got the jobs worked out. I don't think she'll pay any attention to our list here.

Therapist: Hmm. What do Mom and Dad think about that?

Father: Yeah. She's pretty head-strong, that Vicky. I think Teresa's got a point there. Maybe we can have a talk with her first, so she knows she's just making sure things are going according to plan.

Therapist: Who should tell her that, and how?

(The parents look at each other and laugh.)

Mother: Well, I probably ought to do that. Vicky and my husband get into arguments pretty easily. I could explain that she can sort of relax when she comes over, that she doesn't have to do more than just see that things are going according to plan; but she doesn't have to make up the plan.

Therapist: I like that way of describing it. How does the whole family see this? Will this work? Will Aunt Vicky accept this?

STRUCTURE OF PSYCHOTHERAPY SESSIONS
ON A SESSION-BY-SESSION BASIS

A time-limited, problem-specific treatment approach is described. Weekly 1-hour sessions are scheduled; but evaluation sessions may require more time for completing rating scales and computerized administration of the structured interview.

SESSION #1 (EVALUATION)

1. Clarification of presenting problem(s), individually with adolescent, and with relevant family members. This includes determining the young person and his or her family's theories about the presenting problem and its origin.
2. Completion of the Reynolds (1987) or Beck (1978) Depression Inventories and computerized administrations of the Diagnostic Interview for Children and Adolescents (*DSM-IV* version) (DICA-R; Reich et al., 1982).
3. Determination of appropriateness for outpatient therapy versus a need for inpatient or other crisis interventions.
4. Agreement to meet again for further evaluation, as needed.

SESSION #2 (ADOLESCENT)

1. Individual work with young person to clarify and begin educating about the syndrome of depression, using material from DICA-R and rating scales.
2. Identify presence of depression-related conflict areas between the young person and family members.
3. Socialize the young person to a therapeutic framework, including confidentiality versus areas of inclusion of family members.
4. Use of Socratic style to encourage problem-solving mode of treatment in natural environment.
5. Explanation of self-monitoring techniques.
6. Elicit patient feedback about session.
7. Therapist summarizes main issues covered and learned during session.

SESSION #3 (PARENTS AND OTHER FAMILY MEMBERS)

1. Direct inclusion of relevant family members, for purposes of educating family members about issues relating to depression. This also allows the therapist to incorporate the material obtained earlier, regarding what family members tell themselves is the cause of the young person's depressive moods and/or behavior.
2. Mini-lecture regarding depression and automatic thoughts, incorporating parental appraisal of adolescent behavior.
3. Guide interactions between family members toward consensus regarding depression-related areas of conflict.
4. Formulate a treatment contract, centering on resolution of depressive symptoms in young person.
5. Referral of parent(s) for therapy, if mood disorder present for them.

Adolescent

*   Administration of Beck (1978) or Reynolds (1987) Depression Inventories to young person.
*   Provision of reading material (Beck, 1976 or Reinecke, 1992) concerning depression, where appropriate for young person.
*   Elicit feedback.
*   Summarize session.

SESSION #4 (ADOLESCENT)

1. Establish agenda for session.
2. Review reading material (where used), including eliciting patient perceptions of clarity of reading material.
3. Establish target symptoms and problematic life situations. For example, are depressed thinking and mood prominent in particular situations, such as school, parties, or home? The focus must be on the activities and social contexts that seem

to trigger, or elicit, particularly depressed thoughts and affects.

4. Establish links between depressive symptoms, problematic
life situations, and the patient's automatic thoughts.
5. Select beginning treatment focus.
6. Teach self-monitoring strategies.
7. Establish out-of-session assignment, to be carried out in natural environment, and including self-monitoring for presence
of automatic thoughts.
8. Elicit feedback regarding session.
9. Summarize session.

SESSION #5 (ADOLESCENT)

1. Gather information regarding current mood level.
2. Assess emergence of new problems and/or conflicts.
3. Review out-of-session assignment. If patient is unable to report automatic thoughts, teach to detect meaning of problematic situations while reviewing them retrospectively.
4. Set agenda, incorporating any new problems or conflicts.
5. Teach cognitive and/or problem-solving strategies to accomplish session goals.
6. Practice a cognitive or problem-solving strategy, such as the
survey technique, the mood log, or alternative-thinking skills
during session, using real-life example.
7. Out-of-session assignment.
8. Use depression rating scale and provide feedback.
9. Elicit session feedback.
10. Summarize what has been covered and what has been
learned in session.

SESSION #6 (ADOLESCENT)

1. Review out-of-session assignment.
2. Quick review of week.
3. Set agenda.
4. Select target issue.

5. Employ cognitive or problem-solving strategies.
6. Out-of-session assignment.
7. Elicit feedback.
8. Summarize session.

SESSION #7 (ADOLESCENT)

1. Brief review of past week.
2. Review of out-of-session assignment.
3. Set agenda.
4. Select target symptoms or issues.
5. Teach new cognitive or problem-solving technique and apply to real-life situation, such as may have emerged from review of past week. Selecting such situations insures that the patient's focus is on "hot" situations and cognitions that make therapy more cogent and engaging for the young person.
6. Set up out-of-session assignment, employing newly trained techniques for addressing recurring problem situations during the upcoming week.
7. Administer depression scale and review.
8. Elicit feedback about therapy.
9. Summarize session.

SESSION #8 (ADOLESCENT)

1. Review past week.
2. Review homework assignment.
3. Establish agenda for current session.
4. Use role-playing or problem-solving strategies to address problematic situations related to depression.
5. Focus on self-monitoring of automatic thoughts in problematic situations, and develop alternatives to those thoughts.
6. Prepare young person for inclusion of family members in next session by reviewing specific problems on which to work, as well as his or her expectations for change.
7. Elicit session feedback.
8. Summarize session.

SESSION #9 (FAMILY)

1. Provide entire family with rationale and hopes for session's accomplishment, using material from diagnostic phase concerning shared agreement about problem areas needing to be resolved.
2. Develop perspective-taking skills, by encouraging family members to state their own points of view regarding key areas of difficulty related to depression. Problematic areas not related to depression should not be discussed but should be noted for possible later intervention.
3. Use cognitive interventions to encourage family to test use of such distortions as "mind-reading" of each other's motives and inner states.
4. Use problem-solving interventions to help family "brainstorm" alternative solutions, where needed.
5. Development of homework assignment for designated problem resolution.
6. Therapist support for "breakthroughs."
7. Elicit family feedback about session, including focus on any family members who may feel that their side was in any way slighted.
8. Therapist summarizes what has been learned and accomplished in session.

SESSION #10 (FAMILY)

1. Review past session's impact on family.
2. Review homework.
3. Establish agenda for session.
4. Refine strategies for dealing with problem areas in Session #9, or select new problem area.
5. Encourage brainstorming by family.
6. Use problem-solving strategies with family.
7. Homework assignment.
8. Praise family efforts. Encourage return to therapy, as needed.

9. Elicit perceptions of session.
10. Summarize session.

SESSION #11 (ADOLESCENT)

1. Meet with individual young person.
2. Review young person's experience of family session.
3. Set agenda for current session.
4. Explore status of automatic thoughts and current levels of depression.
5. Work on use of cognitive techniques, such as labeling cognitive distortions.
6. Set up homework assignment, involving use of cognitive strategies.
7. Elicit feedback about therapy session.
8. Summarize session.

SESSION #12 (ADOLESCENT)

1. Review prior week.
2. Review homework.
3. Set agenda.
4. Explore psychosocial "triggers" for depressive affect and cognition. Such triggers are the social and/or situational contexts that may elicit depressed thinking and moods.
5. Use cognitive and problem-solving techniques to deal with specific triggering situations.
6. Homework assignment involving one triggering situation.
7. Elicit feedback.
8. Summarize feedback.

SESSION #13 (ADOLESCENT)

1. Review homework assignment.
2. Set agenda.
3. Further explore triggering situations, as well as automatic thoughts and reactions in those situations.

4. Address problem situations, cognitions, and behaviors through role playing.
5. Homework assignment, refining coping strategies with remaining triggering events, and self-monitoring.
6. Elicit feedback from patient about session.
7. Summarize session.

SESSION #14 (ADOLESCENT)

1. Review week.
2. Review homework.
3. Explore remaining family issues with young person.
4. Plan for last family sessions.
5. *Homework:* practice coping cognitions in previously problematic situations and self-monitoring.
6. Elicit feedback.
7. Summarize session.

SESSION #15 (FAMILY)

1. Include family in final problem-solving session.
2. Review progress since last effort.
3. Use problem-solving strategies with family to address any remaining conflicts that are related to young person's depression.
4. Discuss termination issues with family members, including prospects for "booster sessions" in 6 to 12 months, if needed. Because of the prospects that depression may recur, an episodic therapy is advocated. Families and young people need not have relapses of depression resolutely predicted by the therapist. Yet, the therapist should make clear that families and young people often return for further work, as needed. Exploration of the conditions under which such new episodes of therapy might occur *are* in order.
5. *Homework:* help family set up periodic family council meetings to address problems on their own, once therapy ends.
6. Elicit feedback from family.
7. Summarize session.

SESSION #16 (ADOLESCENT)

1. Individual session with young person.
2. Review prior session.
3. Set agenda.
4. Work on relapse identification and prevention procedures.
5. Discuss how therapy can be used to solve daily problems, as well as relapse of depression.
6. *Homework:* use cognitive or problem-solving strategies to solve one miniproblem from daily living.
7. Elicit feedback about session.
8. Summarize session accomplishments.

SESSION #17 (ADOLESCENT)

1. Review homework.
2. Set agenda.
3. Review techniques that young person has found to be most helpful.
4. *Homework:* work on relapse plan, making sure not to forcefully predict relapse, but to help young person have a realistic appraisal of potentially recurrent nature of major depression.
5. Elicit feedback about session.
6. Summarize session accomplishments and what was covered.
7. Readministration of DICA-R.

SESSION #18 (ADOLESCENT)

1. Review homework.
2. Set agenda.
3. Review DICA-R.
4. Further review techniques that patient has found to be helpful during therapy.
5. Patient and therapist provide feedback to one another regarding course of therapy.
6. Summarize overall course of treatment.
7. *Homework:* maintenance of gains from treatment.

8. Give therapeutic certificate.
9. Reassure about availability of future services, as needed.

FINAL COMMENTS

Adolescent depression continues to pose serious challenges to our society and to the therapists who work with young people. While cognitive therapy has shown considerable promise as a treatment for adult depression, much work remains to adapt cognitive therapy for work with children and adolescents. This guide has aspired to that goal.

At the same time, the nature of the American health care system has undergone dramatic changes during the past 5 to 10 years. These changes are deeply affecting the delivery of mental health services, and the future of such services remains uncertain (N. A. Cummings, Pallak, & J. L. Cummings, 1996). The rapid growth of managed care has involved a focus on cost-containment, with issues of quality often subordinated to issues of money. Therapists are challenged as never before to develop treatment models that are rationally and empirically grounded, that can demonstrate a commitment to measured outcomes, and that recognize the financial constraints impinging on practitioners, patients, payers, and health plans.

The focus of this guide is consistent with the current trend towards time-effective treatment (Budman, 1995). The characteristics of such treatments include:

1. A problem and/or diagnosis-specific focus.
2. An action orientation, demanding patient effort to succeed.
3. A strong focus on the treatment relationship, to encourage patient collaboration in the change process.
4. A focus on time, with treatment intended to address episodes of specific disorder(s) and/or problems.
5. An emphasis on spelling out the premises of one's treatment, and subjecting those treatments to empirical scrutiny.

It is hoped that market forces and good standards of practice will eventually meet, creating new treatments that are, above all else, helpful to young people suffering from depression and other affective disorders. I would like to think that this work contributes to that effort.

REFERENCES

Achenbach, T. M., & Edelbrock, C. (1983). *Manual for the Child Behavior Checklist and Revised Child Behavior Profile.* Burlington: Department of Psychiatry, University of Vermont.

Barkley, R. (1990). *Attention Deficit Hyperactivity Disorder.* New York: Guilford.

Beach, S. R. H., Sandeen, E. E., & O'Leary, K. D. (1990). *Depression in Marriage.* New York: Guilford.

Beck, A. T. (1976). *Cognitive Therapy and the Emotional Disorders.* New York: New American Library.

Beck, A. T. (1978). *Depression Inventory.* Philadelphia: Center for Cognitive Therapy.

Beck, A. T., & Greenberg, R. (1976). *Coping With Depression.* Philadelphia: Philadelphia Center for Cognitive Therapy.

Beck, A. T., Rush, A. J., Shaw, B. F., & Emery, G. (1979). *Cognitive Therapy of Depression.* New York: Guilford.

Beck, A. T., & Young, J. E. (1985). Depression. In D. H. Barlow (Ed.), *Clinical Handbook of Psychological Disorders* (pp. 206-244). New York: Guilford.

Biglan, A., Hops, H., Sherman, L., Friedman, L. S., Arthur, J., & Osteen, V. (1985). Problem solving interactions of depressed women and their husbands. *Behavior Therapy, 16,* 431-451.

Birmaher, B., Ryan, N. D., Williamson, D. E., Brent, D. A., & Kaufman, J. (1996). Childhood and adolescent depression: A review of the past 10 years. Part II. *Journal of the American Academy of Child and Adolescent Psychiatry, 35*(12), 1575-1583.

Boszormenyi-Nagy, I. (1987). *The Foundations of Contextual Therapy: The Collected Papers of Ivan Boszormenyi-Nagy.* New York: Brunner/Mazel.

Boszormenyi-Nagy, I., Grunebaum, J., & Ulrich, D. (1991). Context therapy. In A. S. Gurman & D. Kniskern (Eds.), *The Handbook of Family Therapy* (pp. 200-238). New York: Brunner/Mazel.

Boszormenyi-Nagy, I., & Krasner, B. R. (1986). *Between Give and Take: A Clinical Guide to Contextual Therapy.* New York: Brunner/Mazel.

Boszormenyi-Nagy, I., & Spark, G. M. (1973). *Invisible Loyalties.* New York: Brunner/Mazel.

Bowers, W., & Temple, S. D. (1995). *Supervising in Cognitive Therapy: Supervising Cognitive Therapists from Diverse Fields.* Manuscript submitted for publication.

Braswell, L. (1991). Involving parents in cognitive-behavioral therapy with children and adolescents. In P. C. Kendall (Ed.), *Child and Adolescent Therapy: Cognitive-Behavioral Procedures* (pp. 316-351). New York: Guilford.

Braswell, L., & Kendall, P. C. (1988). Cognitive behavioral methods with children. In K. S. Dobson (Ed.), *Handbook of Cognitive-Behavioral Therapies* (pp. 167-213). New York: Guilford.

Budman, S. (Ed.). (1995). *Forms of Brief Therapy.* New York: Guilford.

Burns, D. D. (1980). *Feeling Good: The New Mood Therapy.* New York: Penguin.

Burns, D. D. (1989). *The Feeling Good Handbook: Using the New Mood Therapy in Everyday Life.* New York: William Morrow and Company.

Cantwell, D. P., Lewinsohn, P. M., Rohde, P., & Seeley, J. R. (1997). Correspondence between adolescent report and parental report of psychiatric diagnostic data. *Journal of the Ameri-*

can Academy of Child and Adolescent Psychiatry, 36(5), 610-619.

Carlson, G. A., & Garber, J. (1986). Developmental issues in the classification of depression in children. In M. Rutter, C. E. Izard, & P. B. Read (Eds.), *Depression in Young People: Developmental and Clinical Perspectives* (pp. 399-434). New York: Guilford.

Carlson, G. A., Kashani, J. H., Thomas, M. F., Vaidya, A., & Daniel, A. E. (1987). Comparison of two structured interviews on a psychiatrically hospitalized population of children. *Journal of the American Academy of Child and Adolescent Psychiatry, 5,* 645-648.

Chandler, M. (1973). Egocentrism and anti-social behavior: The assessment and training of social perspective-taking skills. *Developmental Psychology, 9,* 326-332.

Colapinto, J. (1991). Structural family therapy. In A. S. Gurman & D. P. Kniskern (Eds.), *The Handbook of Family Therapy* (pp. 417-443). New York: Brunner/Mazel.

Cummings, N. A., Pallak, M. S., & Cummings, J. L. (Eds.). (1996). *Surviving the Demise of Solo Practice: Mental Health Practitioners Prospering in the Era of Managed Care.* Madison, WI: Psychosocial Press.

Derogatis, L. R. (1983). *SCL-90: Administration, Scoring and Procedures Manual for the Revised Edition.* Baltimore: Clinical Psychometric Research.

D'Zurilla, T. J. (1988). Problem-solving therapies. In K. S. Dobson (Ed.), *Handbook of Cognitive-Behavioral Therapies* (pp. 85-135). New York: Guilford.

Elkin, I. (1994). The NIMH treatment of depression collaborative research program: Where we began and where we are. In A. Bergin & S. Garfield (Eds.), *The Handbook of Psychotherapy and Behavior Change* (4th ed., pp. 114-142). New York: John Wiley & Sons.

Elson, M., & Kohut, E. (1987). *The Kohut Seminars: On Self Psychology and Psychotherapy With Adolescents and Young Adults.* New York: W. W. Norton.

Fauber, R. L., & Long, N. (1991). Children in context: The role of the family in child psychotherapy. *Journal of Consulting and Clinical Psychology, 59*(6), 813-820.

Fleming, J. E., & Offord, D. R. (1990). Epidemiology of childhood depressive disorders: A critical review. *Journal of the American Academy of Child and Adolescent Psychiatry, 29*(4), 571-580.

Freeman, A. (1987). Cognitive therapy: An overview. In A. Freeman & V. Greenwood (Eds.), *Cognitive Therapy: Applications in Psychiatric and Medical Settings* (pp. 19-35). New York: Human Sciences Press.

Freeman, A., Pretzer, J., Fleming, B., & Simon, K. (1990). *Clinical Applications of Cognitive Therapy.* New York: Plenum.

Garfield, S. L. (1989). *The Practice of Brief Psychotherapy.* Elmsford, NY: Pergamon.

Geller, B. (1991). Commentary on unexplained deaths of children on Norpramin. *Journal of the American Academy of Child and Adolescent Psychiatry, 30*(4), 682.

Guidano, V. F. (1987). *Complexity of the Self: A Developmental Approach to Psychopathology and Therapy.* New York: Guilford.

Guidano, V. F. (1988). A systems, process-oriented approach to cognitive therapy. In K. S. Dobson (Ed.), *Handbook of Cognitive-Behavioral Therapies* (pp. 307-354). New York: Guilford.

Guidano, V. F., & Liotti, G. (1983). *Cognitive Processes and Emotional Disorders.* New York: Guilford.

Gurman, A. S., & Kniskern, D. P. (1991). *The Handbook of Family Therapy.* New York: Brunner/Mazel.

Hammen, C., & Rudolph, K. D. (1996). Childhood depression. In E. J. Mash & R. A. Barkley (Eds.), *Child Psychopathology* (pp. 153-195). New York: Guilford.

Herjanic, B., & Reich, W. (1982). Development of a structured psychiatric interview for children: Agreement between child and parent on individual symptoms. *Journal of Abnormal Child Psychology, 10*(3), 307-324.

Hollon, S. D. (1990). Combined cognitive therapy and pharmacotherapy in the treatment of depression. In D. W. Manning & A. J. Frances (Eds.), *Combined Pharmacotherapy and*

Psychotherapy for Depression (pp. 37-64). Washington, DC: American Psychiatric Press.

Holloway, E. L., & Neufeldt, S. A. (1995). Supervision: Its contributions to treatment efficacy. *Journal of Consulting and Clinical Psychology, 63,* 207-213.

Kashani, J. H., Beck, N. C., Hoeper, E. W., Fallahi, C., Corcoran, C. M., McAllister, J. A., Rosenberg, T. K., & Reid, J. C. (1987). Psychiatric disorders in a community sample of adolescents. *American Journal of Psychiatry, 144,* 584-589.

Kashani, J. H., & Schmid, L. S. (1992). Epidemiology and etiology of depressive disorders. In M. Shafii & S. L. Shafii (Eds.), *Clinical Guide to Depression in Children and Adolescents* (pp. 43-64). Washington, DC: American Psychiatric Press.

Kazdin, A. E. (1989). Childhood depression. In E. J. Mash & R. A. Barkley (Eds.), *Treatment of Childhood Disorders* (pp. 135-166). New York: Guilford.

Kazdin, A. E. (1991). Effectiveness of psychotherapy with children and adolescents. *Journal of Consulting and Clinical Psychology, 59*(6), 785-798.

Kendall, P. C., Cantwell, D. P., & Kazdin, A. E. (1989). Depression in children and adolescents: Assessment issues and recommendations. *Cognitive Therapy and Research, 13*(2), 109-146.

Kendall, P. C., MacDonald, J. P., & Treadwell, K. R. H. (1995). The treatment of anxiety disorders in youth. In A. R. Eisen, C. A. Kearney, & C. E. Shaefer (Eds.), *Clinical Handbook of Anxiety Disorders in Children an Adolescents* (pp. 573-597). New York: Jason Aronson.

Kendall, P. C., & Morris, R. J. (1991). Child therapy: Issues and recommendations. *Journal of Consulting and Clinical Psychology, 59*(6), 777-784.

King, R. A., & Noshpitz, J. D. (1991). *Pathways of Growth: Essentials of Child Psychiatry.* New York: John Wiley & Sons.

Kutcher, S. P., & Marton, P. (1989). Parameters of adolescent depression: A review. *Psychiatric Clinics of North America, 12*(4), 895-918.

LaBruzza, A. L. (1994). *Using DSM-IV: A Clinician's Guide to Psychiatric Diagnosis.* New York: Jason Aronson.

Leslie, L. A. (1988). Cognitive-behavioral and systems models of family therapy: How compatible are they? In N. B. Epstein, S. E. Schlesinger, & W. Dryden (Eds.), *Cognitive-Behavior Therapy With Families* (pp. 49-83). New York: Brunner/Mazel.

Leslie, L. A., & Epstein, N. (1988). Cognitive-behavioral treatment of remarried families. In N. B. Epstein, S. E. Schlesinger, & W. Dryden (Eds.), *Cognitive-Behavior Therapy With Families* (pp. 151-182). New York: Brunner/Mazel.

Lewinsohn, P. M., & Clarke, G. N. (1990). Cognitive-behavioral treatment for depressed adolescents. *Behavioral Therapy, 21,* 301-401.

Liotti, G. (1987). Structural cognitive therapy. In W. Dryden & W. L. Golden (Eds.), *Cognitive-Behavioral Approaches to Psychotherapy* (pp. 92-128). New York: Hemisphere Publishing.

Matson, J. L. (1989). *Treating Depression in Children and Adolescents.* New York: Pergamon.

Minuchin, S. (1974). *Families and Family Therapy.* Cambridge, MA: Harvard University Press.

Minuchin, S., & Fishman, H. C. (1981). *Family Therapy Techniques.* Cambridge, MA: Harvard University Press.

Moos, R. H., & Moos, B. S. (1984). *Family Environment Scale Manual.* Palo Alto, CA: Consulting Psychologists Press.

Moreau, D. L. (1990). Major depression in childhood and adolescence. *Psychiatric Clinics of North America, 13*(2), 355-368.

Moreau, D. L., Mufson, L., Weissman, M., & Klerman, G. (1991). Interpersonal psychotherapy for adolescent depression: Description of modification and preliminary application. *Journal of the American Academy of Child and Adolescent Psychiatry, 30*(4), 642-651.

Mueser, K. T., & Glynn, S. M. (1995). *Behavioral Family Therapy for Psychiatric Disorders.* Needham Heights, MA: Allyn and Bacon.

Mufson, L., Moreau, D. L., Weissman, M., & Klerman, G. (1993). *Interpersonal Psychotherapy for Depressed Adolescents.* New York: Guilford.

Nezu, A. M., Nezu, C. M., & Perri, M. G. (1989). *Problem-Solving Therapy for Depression: Theory, Research and Clinical Guidelines.* New York: John Wiley & Sons.

Nichols, M. (1984). *Family Therapy: Concepts and Methods.* New York: Gardner.

Nichols, M., & Schwartz, R. (1995). *Family Therapy: Concepts and Methods* (3rd ed.). Boston: Allyn and Bacon.

Puig-Antich, J., Lukens, E., Davies, M., Goetz, D., Brennan-Quattrock, K., & Todak, G. (1985a). Psychosocial function in prepubertal major depressive disorders: 1. Interpersonal relationships during the depressive episode. *Archives of General Psychiatry, 42,* 500-507.

Puig-Antich, J., Lukens, E., Davies, M., Goetz, D., Brennan-Quattrock, K., & Todak, G. (1985b). Psychosocial function in prepubertal major depressive disorders: 2. Interpersonal relationships after sustained recovery from affective episode. *Archives of General Psychiatry, 42,* 511-517.

Rapoport, J. L. (1989). *The Boy Who Couldn't Stop Washing.* Washington, DC: American Psychiatric Press.

Rapoport, J. L., & Ismond, D. R. (1990). *DSM-III-R Training Guide for Diagnosis of Childhood Disorders.* New York: Brunner/Mazel.

Reich, W., & Earls, F. (1987). Rules for making psychiatric diagnoses in children on the basis of multiple sources of information: Preliminary strategies. *Journal of Abnormal Child Psychology, 15*(4), 601-616.

Reich, W., Herjanic, B., Welner, Z., & Gandhy, R. P. (1982). Development of a structured psychiatric interview for children: Agreement on diagnosis comparing child and parent interviews. *Journal of Abnormal Child Psychology, 10*(4), 325-336.

Reinecke, M. A. (1992). Cognitive therapy with children: Development adaptations in treating depression and suicide. In A. Freeman & F. Dattilio (Eds.), *Comprehensive Casebook of Cognitive Therapy* (pp. 147-158). New York: Plenum.

Reynolds, W. M. (1987). *Reynolds Adolescent Depression Scale.* San Antonio, TX: Psychological Corporation.

Reynolds, W. M., & Coats, K. I. (1986). A comparison of cognitive-behavioral therapy and relaxation training for the treatment of depression in adolescents. *Journal of Consulting and Clinical Psychology, 54*(5), 633-660.

Robin, A. L., Bedway, M., & Gilroy, M. (1994). Problem-solving communication training. In C. W. LeCroy (Ed.), *Handbook of Child and Adolescent Treatment Manuals* (pp. 92-125). New York: Lexington Books.

Robin, A. L., & Foster, S. L. (1989). *Negotiating Parent-Child Conflict: A Behavioral Family Systems Approach.* New York: Guilford.

Rosenberg, D. R., Holttum, J., & Gershon, S. (1994). *Textbook of Pharmacotherapy for Children and Adolescent Psychiatric Disorders.* New York: Brunner/Mazel.

Rutter, M. (1986). The developmental psychopathology of depression: Issues and perspectives. In M. Rutter, C. E. Izard, & P. B. Read (Eds.), *Depression in Young People: Developmental and Clinical Perspectives* (pp. 3-32). New York: Guilford.

Ryan, N. D. (1992). Pharmacological treatment of major depression. In M. Shafii & S. L. Shafii (Eds.), *Clinical Guide to Depression in Children and Adolescents* (pp. 219-232). Washington, DC: American Psychiatric Press.

Safran, J. D., & Segal, Z. V. (1990). *International Process in Cognitive Therapy.* New York: Basic Books.

Schrodt, G. R. (1992). Cognitive therapy of depression. In M. Shafii & S. L. Shafii (Eds.), *Clinical Guide to Depression in Children and Adolescents* (pp. 197-218). Washington, DC: American Psychiatric Press.

Silverman, W. K. (1994). Structured diagnostic interviews. In T. H. Ollendick, J. J. King, & W. Yule (Eds.), *International Handbook of Phobic and Anxiety Disorders in Children.* New York: Plenum.

Spivack, G., Platt, J. J., & Shure, M. B. (1976). *The Problem-Solving Approach to Adjustment.* San Francisco: Jossey-Bass.

Spivack, G., & Shure, M. B. (1974). *Social Adjustment of Young Children: A Cognitive Approach to Solving Real Life Problems.* San Francisco: Jossey-Bass.

Stark, K. D. (1990). *Childhood Depression: School-Based Intervention.* New York: Guilford

Stark, K. D., Raffaelle, L., & Reysa, A. (1994). The treatment of depressed children: A skills training approach to working with children and families. In C. W. LeCroy (Ed.), *Handbook of Child and Adolescent Treatment Manuals* (pp. 343-398). New York: Lexington Books.

Stark, K. D., Reynolds, W. M., & Kaslow, N. J. (1987). A comparison of the relative efficacy of self-control therapy and a behavioral problem-solving therapy for depression in children. *Journal of Abnormal Child Psychology, 15*(1), 91-113.

Strober, M., McCracken, J., & Hanna, G. (1989). Affective disorders. In L. K. Hsu & M. Hersen (Eds.), *Recent Developments in Adolescent Psychiatry* (pp. 201-232). New York: John Wiley & Sons.

VanHeusden, A., & Van Den Eerenbeemt, E. (1987). *Balance in Motion: Ivan Boszormenyi-Nagy and His Vision of Individual and Family Therapy.* New York: Brunner/Mazel.

Weishaar, M. E., & Beck, A. T. (1987). Cognitive therapy. In W. Dryden & W. L. Golden (Eds.), *Cognitive-Behavioral Approaches to Psychotherapy* (pp. 61-92). New York: Hemisphere Publishing.

Weller, E. B., & Weller, R. (Eds.). (1984). *Major Depressive Disorders in Children.* Washington, DC: American Psychiatric Press.

White, M., & Epston, D. (1990). *Narrative Means to Therapeutic Ends.* New York: W. W. Norton.

Wilkes, T. C. R., Belsher, G., Rush, A. J., Frank, E., & Associates. (1994). *Cognitive Therapy for Depressed Adolescents.* New York: Guilford.

Wilkes, T. C. R., & Rush, A. J. (1988). Adaptations of cognitive therapy for depressed adolescents. *Journal of the American Academy of Child and Adolescent Psychiatry, 27,* 381-386.

Winnicott, D. (1958). *Collected Papers.* London: Tavistock.

Young, J. E. (1994). *Cognitive Therapy for Personality Disorders: A Schema-Focused Approach* (rev. ed.). Sarasota, FL: Professional Resource Press.

If You Found This Book Useful . . .

You might want to know more about our other titles.

If you would like to receive our latest catalog, please return this form:

Name:_____
(Please Print)

Address:_____

Address:_____

City/State/Zip:_____
This is ❑ home ❑ office

Telephone:(_____)_____

I am a:

_____ Psychologist   _____ Mental Health Counselor
_____ Psychiatrist   _____ Marriage and Family Therapist
_____ School Psychologist   _____ Not in Mental Health Field
_____ Clinical Social Worker   _____ Other:_____

◆   ◆   ◆

Professional Resource Press
P.O. Box 15560
Sarasota, FL 34277-1560

Telephone #941-366-7913
FAX #941-366-7971
E-mail at mail@prpress.com

BTA/9/97

Add A Colleague To Our Mailing List . . .

If you would like us to send our latest catalog to one of your colleagues, please return this form.

Name:_____
(Please Print)

Address:_____

Address:_____

City/State/Zip:_____
This is ☐ home ☐ office

Telephone:(_____)_____

This person is a:

_____ Psychologist   _____ Mental Health Counselor
_____ Psychiatrist   _____ Marriage and Family Therapist
_____ School Psychologist   _____ Not in Mental Health Field
_____ Clinical Social Worker   _____ Other:_____

Name of person completing this form:_____

◆   ◆   ◆

Professional Resource Press
P.O. Box 15560
Sarasota, FL 34277-1560

Telephone #941-366-7913
FAX #941-366-7971
E-mail at mail@prpress.com

BTA/9/97